DEVELOPING B2B SOCIAL COMMUNITIES

KEYS TO GROWTH, INNOVATION, AND CUSTOMER LOYALTY

Margaret Brooks

J. J. Lovett

Sam Creek

technologies
PRESS

Developing B2B Social Communities: Keys to Growth, Innovation, and Customer Loyalty

President and Publisher: Paul Manning
Acquisitions Editor: Jeff Olson
Developmental Editor: Robert Hutchinson
Technical Reviewer: Rachel Happe
Editorial Board: Steve Anglin, Mark Beckner, Ewan Buckingham, Gary Cornell, Morgan Ertel,
    Jonathan Gennick, Jonathan Hassell, Robert Hutchinson, Michelle Lowman, James Markham,
    Matthew Moodie, Jeff Olson, Jeffrey Pepper, Douglas Pundick, Ben Renow-Clarke,
    Dominic Shakeshaft, Gwenan Spearing, Matt Wade, Tom Welsh
Coordinating Editor: Rita Fernando
Copy Editor: Terry Kornak
Compositor: SPi Global
Indexer: SPi Global
Cover Designer: Anna Ishchenko

Distributed to the book trade worldwide by Springer Science+Business Media, LLC, 233 Spring Street, 6th Floor, New York, NY 10013. Phone 1-800-SPRINGER, fax (201) 348-4505, e-mail orders-ny@springer-sbm.com, or visit www.springeronline.com.

For information on translations, please e-mail rights@apress.com, or visit www.apress.com.

Apress and friends of ED books may be purchased in bulk for academic, corporate, or promotional use. eBook versions and licenses are also available for most titles. For more information, reference our Special Bulk Sales–eBook Licensing web page at www.apress.com/bulk-sales.

In memory of Rob Rachlin – devoted husband and father, dedicated community manager, valued member of our team, and colleague and friend to many. You have left us too soon and will be missed by all.

Contents

Foreword... vii

About the Authors.. ix

About the Technical Reviewer............................... xi

Acknowledgments xiii

Preface... xv

Chapter 1: The Human Need to Connect....................... 1

Chapter 2: Community as the Centerpiece for Customer
            Engagement....................................... 17

Chapter 3: Community Models................................ 47

Chapter 4: Life Cycle and Maturity Models for Online Communities ... 69

Chapter 5: Community Management............................ 89

Chapter 6: Case Study in Focus: CA Technologies 115

Chapter 7: Business Impact through Community............... 131

Chapter 8: Developing B2B Social Communities 159

Index 183

Foreword

Business-to-business (B2B) organizations have always needed a close relationship with their customers in order to thrive. Customer relationships are essential to repeat business, and online communities enable B2B organizations to better deliver customer-facing functions. Communities can help customers get more value from their products and services; develop better new products and services; market and sell better from a thought leadership platform; and gain control over what the market is saying about the company.

Looking at all these potential benefits, B2B companies often ask whether an online community is right for them. This book will help any organization that has launched or is considering launching an online B2B community to understand what it will take for it to reap the benefits that an online B2B community can confer. It will also help any organization that already has a B2B online community to optimize its return on investment. Focusing on the types of companies that benefit most from online communities and on the three models for online communities—public, private, and hybrid—from which companies may choose, Developing B2B Social Communities shows any company how to choose the best strategy to ensure that their B2B customer community is vibrant and engaged over time and supports the company business goals.

An online community can be a collective stethoscope that offers a company real-time access to the heartbeats of its customers, prospects, suppliers, and employees as they interact with each other asynchronously under the quickening pulse of thought leaders and influencers doing what organizational behaviorist Don Schon calls "reflective practice"—that is, fetching up ordinarily tacit professional knowledge for informal exchange with community members.

But building these evergreen collaboration ecosystems is easier said than done. Success in developing and cultivating B2B online communities depends on clear-sightedness and commitment: a clear understanding of the purpose of the online community; the ability to launch, engage, and create tangible business value with agility; and the organizational willingness and nimbleness to embrace the change that happens when community outcomes impact core business processes. To be truly successful from a business perspective, the information exchanged in communities needs to be effectively channeled to influence research and development processes, product and service launches, and customer care programs.

The authors take readers on a journey of exploration into not just the how but also the why of online B2B communities, identifying the psychological foundation of communities with the basic human need to connect with peers. Readers will find helpful the authors' syntheses of current research and writing in the art and science of community building and their insights into engagement trends such as gamification, creating incentives for experts to participate, methods for keeping members involved, and ways to use the social data within the organization.

Creating a collaborative enterprise is everyone's responsibility. This book will help you make your contribution to the irresistible future in which B2B online communities are the backbone of the connected enterprise.

Vanessa DiMauro
CEO and Founder, Leader Networks, LLC

About the Authors

Margaret Brooks, Senior Advisor, Business Unit Strategy for the Global Presales Organization and former Vice President, Customer Success, joined CA Technologies in 1999. In the Customer Success organization, she was responsible for the development and vitality of the CA global communities representing a cross section of product and solution communities. This team continues to lead transformation programs to improve customer experience and supports the business requirement for continued enhancements to the online customer experience.

In her career at CA Technologies, Brooks has held many executive positions in sales, technical sales, and business development. She has also specialized in governance, risk, and compliance and was involved with thought leadership, publications, and solution development in this area for several years. She published articles in *WSTA* magazine, *KM World*, and *SC Magazine* on the topics of governance, risk, and compliance. She has been nominated for the CEO Award for her contributions in this area.

Brooks draws on more than 35 years of experience in the IT industry. Prior to joining CA, she led consulting engagements at the data warehousing division of Platinum Technologies. Before that, she held management positions in data warehousing and information resource management, focusing primarily on companies in the healthcare and insurance areas. She holds a Bachelor of Science degree in Health Education from the University of Alabama.

J. J. Lovett, Director, Community Programs at CA Technologies, has over 15 years of experience in online collaborative technology and community building. He has built many online collaborative communities for both internal and B2B organizations and across several industries. He has used his military background and varied experience to develop a pragmatic approach to people, systems, and collaborative concepts that translates across different industries and environments. Starting at CA Technologies a decade ago, he has played a pivotal role in the transition from in-person to online interaction for the company's customers and partners. Having helped pioneer the role of online community manager at CA Technologies, he now leads both the community management and operations teams that enable the more than 40 online communities and more than 175 regional user groups around the globe. He is a proud husband and father, an avid boater, an eager novice in the kitchen, and part-time adventure racer.

Sam Creek is a Senior Principal Business Analyst on the CA Communities team at CA Technologies. He works with the MyCA professional networking platform team. Creek has been involved with the development of communities and social media strategies for CA customers and employees for the past four years. Before that, he provided support for the CA Advanced Configuration Manager and the CA Configuration Management Database (CMDB) and was a member of the team that introduced Spectrum Automation Manager. Creek joined CA Technologies in 2007. He previously worked at Cendura, Inc., as the manager of customer support. Prior to that, he was a product manager at Intellisync (now Nokia) for its rapid application development platform for mobile devices. Creek holds a master's degree from the University of Toronto in the History and Philosophy of Science.

About the Technical Reviewer

Rachel Happe has spent the last 15 years helping organizations implement emerging technologies to advance their business strategies.

She understands how networked communications environments can transform how people work, their productivity and their personal satisfaction by aligning their passions, skills, and relationships.

Happe co-founded The Community Roundtable to support business leaders developing their community and social business strategies. Clients including SAP, Aetna, BASF, CA, H&R Block, and CSC benefit from her ability to make sense of abstract trends and to see the implications that technical and operational decisions can have on people and processes.

Happe has served as a product executive at Mzinga, Bitpass, and IDe and as IDC's first analyst covering social technologies. She started her business career as an analyst at PRTM. Connect with her on Twitter at @rhappe.

Acknowledgments

Special thanks go to the CA Technologies Communities team and our Community Leaders, whose dedication to communities and successful efforts gave me the courage to consider sharing our experiences and writing this book. Without my co-authors J. J. and Sam, this book would not have been possible. You both bring many talents to the team and drive toward continued excellence, for which I am grateful.

I want to thank my husband, Jim, for your patience, support, and encouragement throughout my career and while writing this book. I thank my wonderful children, Lauren and Justin, for always being understanding and supportive of me and my work.

—Margaret Brooks

There are too many people to mention when saying thank you to those who helped turn this hobby into a career and my experience into many of the words and concepts in this book. The CA Technologies Communities Team has included many great people and evolved greatly over the 8 years I have been working on this community-engagement venture. So has the group of external community advocates who serve as the board officers and leaders of our communities. Fold in all the intelligent and collaborative individuals across our company who have supported and contributed to our efforts and successes, and a large and diverse assembly of exceptional people is conjured before my mind's eye. Thank you all!

Personally, I offer my sincerest love and appreciation to my wife, Allison, my two fantastic daughters, Juliana and Keira, for supporting my efforts, tolerating my rants, and accepting my need to ship them off to our wonderfully caring and supportive family when I needed to write. I'm also going to throw a fist–paw bump to our semi-wonder mutt, Stormie, for being the gentle ear and eyes when I would read aloud my drafts—and for being patient while waiting to go for a walk.

—J. J. Lovett

Inspiration for this book came directly from the great people we work with at CA Technologies and all of the people who are members of the online CA Communities. I would like to acknowledge especially the Community Leaders who have helped us push the limits of what we can accomplish with a business-focused community.

On a personal level, I want to thank my wife Birgit for the support, patience, and encouragement she has given me throughout this process. I'll also thank Boo the dog and Finn the cat who have served admirably as my trusted advisors and schedule keepers.

—Sam Creek

From all three of us:

Thank you to Robert Hutchinson and Rita Fernando and the Apress team for your patience, your assistance in answering questions, driving us to stay on track, and superb editing to make this book cohesive and to harmonize the voices of three authors. We owe debts of gratitude to Karen Sleeth, who was always there to guide us through the process and encourage us along the way, and to Alma Siedlecki who took over as our reviewer in the middle of the writing and embraced the role at full gallop, never skipping a beat.

We appreciate the input and support from Rachel Happe and Vanessa DiMauro throughout our writing. Both Rachel and Vanessa are experts in their field and have a lot to share regarding the building of online communities. As a leading B2B online community expert, Vanessa was instrumental in helping us decide to write this book. The insights and findings in her articles and blogs inspired us with confidence that we were on the right track. Both Rachel and Vanessa are forward thinkers. We encourage you to follow them to learn what you can do better today and how your communities can become an integral part of social business world of the future.

Preface

J. J.'s, Sam's, and my community journeys began from different perspectives and at different times. The beginnings of many CA Technologies communities preceded all of us. Some of them are independent user associations that have existed over 30 years. Others are local user groups sponsored by CA Technologies. Although these groups were not officially called *communities* at their inception, they were the vanguard of what today we call our online communities. My personal experience with them began as a customer with my participation in Metadata Repository user groups and in an earlier role at CA Technologies, working to develop a new product community. A few years ago, I moved into a new role and was given the privilege of leading the Community team. We are fortunate to have a dedicated and talented team of professional community managers and operations support to help our communities evolve and mature.

When I first joined the team, it was an important time for our communities. We were moving to a new online platform bringing all of our online communities together for the first time on our ca.com platform. New members could more easily find the communities on our website and all members could now reach other users across the globe and get to know a much broader and diverse group of people. Even though our communities had been around for a long time, the visibility of the communities within the company could be improved. As our program continued, we worked diligently to promote and educate our own employees about the communities, resulting in their much greater participation. Now many employees share their expert knowledge and interact with community members around the world. Social media were coming to the forefront within companies, and we already had a great start with our online communities on a single platform. In addition, our executives were also paying attention! Communities are now playing a bigger and bigger role in defining the customer experience and for many are an increasingly vital source of how-to information for our members and of customer intelligence for us. We hope your community journey will be rewarding and our experiences will help you to evolve and lead vibrant and successful B2B communities.

—Margaret Brooks

The Human Need to Connect

Pop quiz!

Imagine you are the lead on an online product community project and you are called into a meeting with the executive steering committee to justify your community business plan. How do you justify your project?

You could focus on:

- **ROI.** Pull together projected numbers on return on investment and cost savings due to support-call deflection and social-sharing conversion rates for sales.

- **Competition.** Say: "Our biggest competitors already have thriving product communities and they are talking about our products on their sites. We need to control the conversation."

- **Staying current.** Social networking is huge! It is quantifiably the biggest thing to hit the Web since, well, the Web. Facebook has several hundred million users. As Google CEO Eric Schmidt put it, "Every two days now we create as much information as we did from the dawn of civilization up until 2003."[1] Almost all of that data is user generated. Tell the steering committee: "By not reaching out and participating in this communications revolution, the company risks being left behind or forgotten."

---

[1]Siegler, MG. "Eric Schmidt: Every 2 Days We Create as Much Information as We Did Up to 2003," TechCrunch, August 4, 2010, http://techcrunch.com/2010/08/04/schmidt-data/.

Though none of these justifications is incorrect none gets to the heart of why supporting online communities is essential. Or rather, they are all correct but are missing the spirit that animates them. What if you simply just said, instead, that the fact your customers are human alone validates your initiative?

It seems obvious that your customers are human (though not always[2]), what does that have to do with justifying building a community around your products? Everything. Humans are by nature social and group themselves together in various levels of communities to achieve their goals. All complex human endeavors are the result of groups of people collaborating in communities: whether it is building skyscrapers or temples, inventing the next disruptive technology, playing in the NFL, learning in schools, eating in restaurants, shopping in stores, or idolizing pop stars, humans love (and need) to gather together.

Remember   Humans are most successful when they collaborate, whether in business, sports, religion, or any other area of life.

Even if we limit our view to the business world, we see that all products and services are the result of communities. Building a product requires a designer, a product manager, a project manager, skilled workers to build it, testers to ensure quality, marketers to let people know about it, salespeople to sell it, and support agents to fix it if it breaks. These are, essentially, members of "communities of purpose" with specific goals relating to the development, production, sale, and maintenance of the product. In this example, multiple layers of communities interact to produce a result.

Even one-of-a-kind artisan products, produced by single person, are the result of a community: the artist learned the skills from small communities such as schools or businesses where the artist served as an apprentice to a master. The larger community dictates the form and function; it has agreed on standards and conventions, and the product itself becomes available to an even larger community made up of an audience that appreciates the work and maybe buys it.

The basis of community and its relation to human endeavor extends to scientific facts, industry standards, and all institutions and economies—in fact, it is often what defines truth. What's more, a person's relationship to a community is multilayered and additive. Each member can belong to several communities,

---

[2]With actual birds (@hungry_birds) and refrigerators tweeting (www.cnn.com/2011/TECH/innovation/01/07/internet.connected.appliances/index.html) and personalized bots creating their own tumblr pages (www.weavrs.com/find/), it is getting harder and harder to make the assumption that everyone you meet on the Internet is a human.

and by joining a new one, it (usually) has no effect on the previous memberships. Each of us, for example, belongs to communities comprised of our immediate and extended families, our local neighborhood or town, our state or province, fellow workers, alumni associations, multiplayer online gaming servers, and so forth.

From the Political Animal to the Social

There are a few ways to begin examining just how fundamental communities are for us. Let's begin with the "why?" and start with one of the earliest investigators into the nature of humanity and the world we inhabit, the Greek philosopher Aristotle. In roughly 350 BC, Aristotle described people as political animals because of our command of language and rational ordering of social bonds. In *Politics* he wrote:[3]

> When several villages are united in a single complete community, large enough to be nearly or quite self-sufficing, the state comes into existence for the sake of a good life. And therefore, if the earlier forms of society are natural, so is the state, for it is the end of them and the nature of a thing is in its end. For what each thing is when fully developed, we call its nature, whether we are speaking of a man, a horse or a family. Besides, the final cause and end of a thing is the best, and to be self-sufficing is the end and the best. Hence it is evident that the state is a creation of nature, and that man is by nature a political animal.
>
> Now, that man is more a political animal than bees or any other gregarious animals is evident. Nature, as we often say, makes nothing in vain, and man is the only animal whom she has endowed with the gift of speech. And whereas mere voice is but an indication of pleasure and pain... the power of speech is intended to set forth the expedient and inexpedient, and therefore likewise the just and the unjust. And it is a characteristic of man that he alone has any sense of good and evil, of just and unjust ... and the association of living beings who have this sense makes a family and a state.

Aristotle identified the notion of community—the bonds between people that form the foundation of a city or a household—as a fundamental aspect of being human.

---

[3]Aristotle. *Politics* (1252b30–1253a3, 1253a8), *The Basic Works of Aristotle*, trans. Richard McKeon (Random House, 1941).

The emphasis on the nature of communication as a cornerstone of these partnerships is a notion that has driven philosophical enquiry from antiquity to the 21st century. In *Philosophical Investigations* Ludwig Wittgenstein posited that language itself works only in a social context. Language has no meaning outside of communicating. This is an obvious point, but it explains how fundamental the notion of community, of social context, is to thinking itself. For example, one of the concepts that Wittgenstein is famous for is "language games"—which serve to illustrate that meaning does not exist on its own in language but only in relation to the actions of those using it and in the mutual recognition among the players of the game[4]:

> *The language is meant to serve for communication between a builder A and an assistant B. A is building with building-stones: there are blocks, pillars, slabs and beams. B has to pass the stones, in the order in which A needs them. For this purpose they use a language consisting of the words "block," "pillar," "slab," "beam." A calls them out;—B brings the stone which he has learnt to bring at such-and-such a call. Conceive this as a complete primitive language.*

This works for any group of people who begin to create specialized meanings for their words in order to communicate, irrespective of whether they are specialized industry terms or inside jokes. Each of these various games can delineate a community based on who understands the terms of the language in a specific way. But is communication the only way to define community? Are communities defined only by common language or common understanding?

In 1887, the German sociologist and philosopher Ferdinand Tonnies—one of the founders of sociology—drew attention to the importance of community and society in his seminal work, *Gemeinschaft und Gesellschaft*. Tonnies said *Gemeinschaft*—community—is the association or set of common bonds that draws together individuals into something that is greater than its parts. *Gesellschaft*—society—on the other hand has to do with an individual's place in relation to others, such as in his or her social status. The rules that govern community are implicit and thrust upon an individual as mores and values that are shared with those around him or her. The rules that govern society are explicit; an individual chooses to behave in a certain way to attain a specific status in relation to others.

Here we have found an interesting departure from the previous descriptions of community, which hinged on the importance of language. Now community has an aspect that is important for the individual. Each part that makes up the whole can have a vested interest beyond just the circumstance that the

---

[4]Wittgenstein, Ludwig. *Philosophical Investigations* (P. M. S. Hacker and Joachim Schulte, Eds., 4th ed.). Hoboken, NJ: Wiley-Blackwell, 2009.

individual has been placed in. As the founder of utilitarianism Jeremy Bentham put it: "It is in vain to talk of the interest of the *community*, without understanding what is the interest of the individual."[5]

Hardwired to Socialize

There was much conjecture at play with these philosophic formulations of community and the individual's relation to it. Let's take it one step further and look at the very building blocks of what it means to be a social being, to be a human. Peeling back those layers, we find neurotransmitters (Figure 1-1) are responsible for how we act, respond, and formulate our thoughts. The interplay between these chemicals is responsible for our various states of mind, memories, feelings, intuitions, and rationalizations. Neurotransmitters include a host of chemicals that transmit signals between the synapses of the neurons in our brains. There are more than 50 different neurochemical messengers that affect various states based on their abundance or depletion. How are they regulated? It depends on the situation—everything from eating to exercising to sleeping affects the amounts that are produced in the brain.

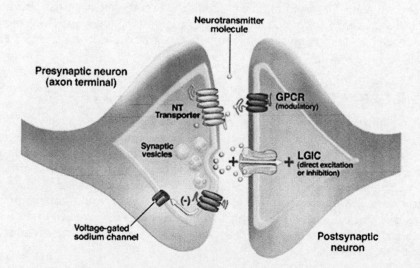

Figure 1-1. A model of how neurotransmitters interact between the axons and dendrites between two brain cells[6]

[5]Bentham, Jeremy. *An Introduction to the Principles of Morals and Legislation* (Oxford: Clarendon Press, 1907).

[6]Lovinger, David M. (2008). "Communication Networks in the Brain." *Alcohol Research & Health* 31(3): 196–214.

The neurotransmitters each correspond to specific receptors that govern various functions in the brain that in turn govern various systems throughout the body. Some of these are very well known, such as endorphins, which reward us with pleasurable feelings by binding to opioid receptors in the brain after, for example, strenuous exercise, resulting in the well-known "runner's high." Another is serotonin, which regulates sleep, muscle contractions, and even mood. Prozac elevates moods by preventing serotonin from being recycled by the brain's waste collection system, thereby keeping a steady supply flowing and preventing depletion to the point depression sets in. There are less famous neurotransmitters as well, like the ominously named Substance P, which transmits pain between our neurons.

The two neurotransmitters that we are going to focus on are dopamine and oxytocin. Dopamine is crucial to several brain functions and plays a huge part in the brain's reward system. Dopamine imbalances are linked to schizophrenia, Parkinson's disease, and attention-deficit hyperactive disorder (ADHD). Dopamine is a key part of how and why we are social beings. The other neurotransmitter is oxytocin—the "love chemical" or "moral molecule," as some researchers are calling it.[7] Oxytocin was first linked to the bonding between mother and child after childbirth but it has since been linked to a number of behaviors from calmness and relaxation to anxiety. It has also been linked to the tendency of humans to group together to form a social group or tribe based on common values for common goals.[8] Is this beginning to sound familiar?

Updating the Status of Your Nucleus Accumbens

Let's begin with dopamine. Dopamine regulates a pathway through your brain to the nucleus accumbens (Figure 1-2), more commonly referred to as your pleasure center. The function of this part of the brain has been studied extensively, and dopamine plays a role in telling the brain when to reward someone for a certain behavior. This fires when you are expecting results that are not predictable, like watching sports or when people give you a compliment. It turns out that this also drives people to talk about themselves, to update statuses, or tweet about events in their lives. In a recent study, the researchers found the following:[9]

[7]Zak, Paul J. *Moral Molecule*. New York: Dutton, 2012.

[8]De Dreu, C. K., Greer, L. L., Van Kleef, G.A., Shalvi, S., and Handgraaf, M. J. (2011). "Oxytocin promotes human ethnocentrism." *Proceedings of the National Academy of Sciences of the USA*, 108(4): 1262–1266. doi:10.1073/pnas.1015316108. PMC 3029708. PMID 21220339.

[9]Tamir, Diana I., and Mitchell, Jason P. (2012). "Disclosing information about the self is intrinsically rewarding." *Proceedings of the National Academy of Sciences of the USA*, 109(21): 8038–8043.

> To the extent that humans are motivated to propagate the products of their minds, opportunities to disclose one's thoughts should be experienced as a powerful form of subjective reward. Here, across five studies, we used a combination of neuroimaging and cognitive methods to demonstrate empirical support for this possibility.

They found that 30% of typical human conversation consisted of talking about one's experiences, but in social media that was closer to 80%.

The highway for dopamine through the brain or mesolimbic pathway goes both ways, though. Dopamine rewards more than just the outward-bound message. It rewards you when you see statuses from others. It rewards you when you find new content. It turns out that dopamine is essential for human survival by laying down the pathways for us to know when and what to eat, when to sleep, and what is pleasurable. Part of what underlies these survival instincts is the brain's ability to reward-seeking behavior with dopamine. Dopamine helps us find food by rewarding us when we find the object of our search. In a similar manner, it rewards us when we log in to Facebook and see what our friends have been up to, what new events are coming up, and who has liked our statuses.[10] In fact, recent research is suggesting that rather than being just about the goal, the "seeking behavior" is itself the reward and that this can set up dopamine loops promoting the interaction between the hunt and the goal.[11] This loop is what happens when we check in "just for a minute" to see what's happening on Reddit and look up an hour later after about 500 clicks.

---

[10]Saadat, Victoria. (2012). "The dopamine high: From social networking to survival." *UScience Review,* 2(2).

[11]Berridge, Kent C., and Robinson, Terry E. (1998). "What is the role of dopamine in reward: Hedonic impact, reward learning, or incentive salience?" *Brain Research Reviews* 28: 309–369.

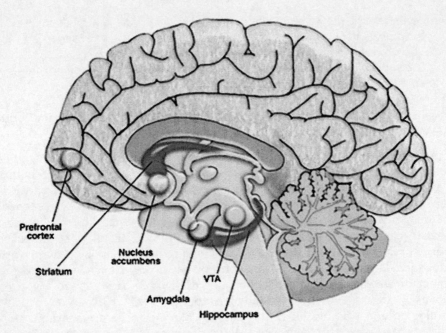

Figure 1-2. The location of nucleus accumbens, also known as the pleasure center of the brain[12]

As you've probably guessed, dopamine does have its downside. It is at the root of most addictions.[13] This is something to keep in mind when you are designing systems to reward users for specific actions.

In light of what we have just discussed about dopamine and innate reward-seeking behavior, how can we make online communities that align with these behaviors? Giving customers the proper platform and venue, with the right amounts of new content for them to consume, will encourage customers to talk about their experiences with your product. Customers can begin to work through issues with each other and provide a source of trustworthy references. They will do so because it is intrinsically rewarding. It is built into the reward center in their brains.

New site content will stimulate dopamine and reinforce customers' perception of your site as a useful resource. Provide the pathways to find the content, along with the ability to search and navigate, because those actions will be naturally reinforced.

---

[12]Clapp, Peter, Bhave, Sanjiv V., and Hoffman, Paula L. (2008). "How Adaptation of the Brain to Alcohol Leads to Dependence." *Alcohol Research & Health* 31(4): 310–339.
[13]Koob, George F. (1992). "Dopamine, addiction and reward." *Seminars in Neuroscience*, 4(2): 139–148.

Trusting the Crowd

Oxytocin—sometimes referred to as the "cuddle chemical"—gets a great deal of attention because it seems to be the neurotransmitter behind our feelings of belonging and our ability to create bonds. It first came to attention as playing a role in the way the mothers bonded with their newborns, but since then, researchers have begun to explore its role in the variety of ways that humans connect with one another.

Dr. Paul J. Zak at Claremont Graduate University has been researching the role oxytocin plays in neuroeconomics. Specifically, he specializes in how the abundance or depletion of this chemical in our brains affects our economic decisions. Zak's research focuses on oxytocin and its ability to increase bonds based on trust, with a specific case being the role in the trust people give to others in online social networks.[14] Zak measured the amounts of oxytocin in their blood before and after spending 10 minutes on Twitter and found that their oxytocin had risen 13.2 percent.[15]

Results of a Pew Research Center study support Zak's hypothesis that these social networks build general as well as site-specific trust. People who visit Facebook many times each day are 43 percent more likely than non-Facebook Internet users are three times more likely than people who don't use the Internet at all to report feeling that most people can be trusted.

Zak maintains that oxytocin is a wonder chemical that acts both as a "social glue" and "economic lubricant."[16] He calls it the "moral molecule" because of its role behind the scenes in human interaction. Its role in social bonding has even been linked to the ability to heal from injuries faster![17]

The effects of neurotransmitters and their chemical cousins the neuro-modulators are due to their abundance or scarcity in the brain at particular junctions. And, as we found with dopamine, oxytocin has a darker side. Examples are jealousy and anger. As mentioned previously, oxytocin plays a

---

[14]Penenberg, Adam L. "Social Networking Affects Brains Like Falling in Love." 2010 July/August, Fast Company. Available at: www.fastcompany.com/1659062/social-networking-affects-brains-falling-love.
[15]Hampton, Keith N. Sessions Goulet, Lauren, Rainie, Lee, and Purcell, Kirsten. "Social Networking Sites and Our Lives." Pew Research Center's Internet & American Life Project, June 6, 2011.
[16]Pendenberg, Adam L. "Digital Oxytocin: How Trust Keeps Facebook, Twitter Humming." July 11, 2011. Available at: www.fastcompany.com/1767125/digital-oxytocin-how-trust-keeps-facebook-twitter-humming.
[17]Gouin, J. P., Carter, S., Pournajafi-Nazarloo, H., Glaser, R., Malarkey, W. B., Loving, T. J., Stowell, J., and Kiecolt-Glaser, J. K. (2010). "Marital behavior, oxytocin, vasopressin, and wound healing." *Psychoneuroendocrinology*, 35(7): 1082–1090. doi: 10.1016/j.psyneuen.2010.01.009. PMC 2888874. PMID 20144509.

role in creating tribal bonds. It can also spawn xenophobia. Think of it this way—the same neurotransmitter that's responsible for creating a team is also responsible for creating an angry mob. The same thing that is responsible for bonding between people is also behind the feelings of possessiveness about that person leading to jealousy.[18] It can even be quite nuanced. Oxytocin, for example, is behind the pleasure we sometimes get in seeing others fail (*Schadenfreude*).[19] In the end, oxytocin is working behind the scenes to give people the ability to pull together against the odds or band together to "rage against the machine."

What does it mean for your business that people are hardwired to bond together, that they find one another trustworthy when they can communicate in a supportive way online? In his popular book, *Speed of Trust*, Stephen Covey describes 13 behaviors by which leaders in an organization can build trust within their organization or with their customers and in so doing close sales and other deals faster.[20] These behaviors include honesty, transparency, and showing loyalty. They are the hallmark behaviors associated with creating social bonds, behaviors fueled by oxytocin.

Keep this in mind as you set up platforms that encourage collaboration and teamwork. You are setting the stage for your customers to create a tribe around your products. The bonds the tribe creates between you and your customers creates an effective competitive barrier. By increasing their ability to communicate and collaborate, you will be increasing their loyalty to your products and brand. But beware—this can have its dark side. Building strong bonds can turn your happy community into an ugly mob when things go wrong. Your failures can quickly become targets for their gallows humor. To prevent such situations from escalating, it's worth returning to those behaviors Covey discusses and directly assesses the situation realistically, openly, and often.

■ **Remember** Dopamine encourages reward-seeking behavior in people and oxytocin reinforces bonds. Together they drive social interaction among the people in your community.

By understanding that each individual in a community has needs that are driven and reinforced by his or her neurochemistry, and that neurochemistry has evolved to drive cooperation, you can gain a deeper understanding about

---

[18]Miller, Greg. (2010). "The Prickly Side of Oxytocin." *Science*, 328(5984): 1343. doi: 10.1126/science.328.5984.1343-a.
[19]Shamay-Tsoory, S. G., Fischer, M., Davash, J., Harari, H., Perach-Bloom, N., and Levkowitz, Y. (2009). "Intranasal administration of oxytocin increases envy and schadenfreude (gloating)." *Biological Psychiatry*, 66(9): 864–870. doi: 10.1016/j.biopsych.2009.06.009.
[20]Covey, Stephen M. R. *The Speed of Trust*. New York: Free Press, 2008.

what is motivating your customers. Combining the reward loops from the dop-amine pathways to encourage self-disclosure, and rewarding-seeking behavior leads to the bonds and loyalty generated by oxytocin, results in a powerful cocktail of neurotransmitters inside of each of your community members that will keep it buzzing along in a beneficial cycle.

We Can Rebuild Him. We Have the Technology… Better…Stronger…Faster.

There is one more reason why "because our customers are humans" makes sense as a justification for a project to build an online community: the speed of technology. Advances in technology and revolutions in communication go hand in hand with what we are learning about how the human brain is hardwired. The reward loops that drive our seeking behavior intensify when the speed of communication increases. That communication becomes more and more valuable because it enables trust in others and breaks down provincial walls. This has revolutionized business in the last few decades as we have gone from disparate local economies based on brick-and-mortar locations to global enterprises accessible 24/7 from any Internet-connected device. There was a point in the not-too-distant past when you would walk into a bookstore and your options were limited to what you saw on the shelves. For better or worse, that has changed. The genie that now allows you immediately to bring up the Amazon app on your iPhone and order any book in print—or even any out of print book that's for sale—is never going back in the bottle. We are not wired for going backward. Each technological advance succeeds and is reinforced as it extends and complements the ways we are already wired to behave.

An interesting pattern emerges with each revolution in communication. At first, newly introduced products are thought of as novelties or toys. Then they begin to gain users and come to be seen as distractions. Later, things reach a tipping point and a device becomes an indispensable tool for getting work done. Eventually, it begins to be supplanted by the next big thing in ultrafast communication and it becomes the formal communication system, embodying what it replaced.

E-mail is a perfect example of this. It began as a system of communication between offices for a very specialized set of people and then became a novel form of communication on the nascent Internet. As it became more popular in the workplace, employers began to see it as a distraction that was inter-rupting their workers' day. Eventually it overtook letters, memos, and voice-mails to become the dominant form of work communication. Then instant messaging began creeping up on its turf and e-mail began to be regulated to more formal kinds of communication that provided an audit trail. Again we can interpret this as dopamine rewarding the early adopters and oxytocin driving more trust between the ever-growing populations of e-mail users until it became the established form of communication. Then something new came along and dopamine loops began rewarding the early adopters who switched over to instant messaging.

Back in the Conference Room

Let's go back and look at the arguments in more detail—besides the best one, that we're all humans—used to justify an investment in online product communities. The ideas we have just been discussing—Aristotle's social animal, neurochemical hardwiring, and the speed of technology—have all been put on the table to justify the simple answer to the question that was posed in the beginning: How do you justify the expenditure for an online product community project? What about the other options? Can we apply what we've learned about community and communication, reward and bonding, and the speed of technology to those options?

Return on Investment

Measuring outcomes and returns for a project gives you a baseline of understanding your success. Just focusing on the numbers may not be enough if you don't understand the mechanism moving the numbers in a particular direction or understand the value of what you are measuring. For example, if your performance indicators are based around answers to questions in a message board, but your support organization takes all of the questions offline and neither it nor the original poster posts the answer back, then technically the question has been answered. But the helpful content isn't being communicated to the community at large. In this case, the measurement for return on investment, based on the number of calls that have been deflected by answers in the community, is misleading and doesn't reflect the value of the community.

Instead, it is important to understand why your key performance indicators are key. Are you generating value for your customers? Are your customers finding it rewarding to visit the site? Are they feeling a sense of accomplishment when they help another customer and answer a question or contribute to a thread? Is the mesolimbic pathway flowing with dopamine? Are the interactions that are happening on the site fostering the sense of community, of building a tribe around your products? Do your customers associate your site with being a community they belong to? Will that lead them to recommend your product? Will that increase in the oxytocin translate into a higher "net promoter" score?

Of course analytics and measurements of success are important to your success. Demonstrating the return on your company's investment will most likely end up justifying your budget. Later in the book we will dig into what is important to measure and why. It may help to explain why you choose the indicators you do if you keep in mind the notions about why they should be moving, why they are creating value, and why they are measuring your success.

Competition

If you have customers, you have a community. If you have a community you have members who want to express themselves (dopamine!) and talk to other members. They are going to band together for or against your brand (oxytocin!). This is going to happen whether you provide a forum for these conversations or not. Although it is an important justification to want to be able to have some control over those conversations, this is really just the beginning of the competitive advantages that providing these tools to your existing community affords you. Let's think about what our neurochemical friends do inside each of your customers and how that can give your brand an edge.

Providing a place for your community gives you the opportunity to increase the cadence of communication with your customers. Giving them new information about your products, tips and tricks, glimpses of your future roadmap—and asking them outright what they think—will create a rewarding bond between your customers and your brand. Interacting with your customers instead of broadcasting at them allows personal relationships to sprout up, and this in turn increases the trust your customers have in your company. Suddenly, your brand isn't some nameless monolithic company but a band of individuals working together with the customer to create the best experience possible around your product.

This creates loyal customers. Moving to a competitor isn't just about moving to a different product, but now it means moving to a different community. It means buying products from strangers who will need to prove they can earn customer's trust. Suddenly the value of your product has shifted from the product itself to relationships with the people who create, build, maintain, and use that product.

New Technologies and the Rise of Social Media

Online social networking isn't just huge in terms of content and membership; it's huge in terms of the revolution that is happening with human communication. Throughout history, changes in technology used to communicate have driven the world forward in terms of technology, science, and trade. From printing to telegraphs, telephones to terminals, e-mail to Twitter, each technological step has increased the speed of cultural transformation. Each change leaves outdated and irrelevant institutions and companies littered in its wake. Each change gives new ideas, trends, companies, and products an opportunity to become the next big thing.

As mentioned before, by definition, humans are social creatures. We are also defined by our use of technology. When these two characteristics are combined, it accelerates all of humanity. We are hardwired to respond positively or negatively to these changes. As we are beginning to discover, the rise in technologies that engender new forms of communication are utilizing the very elements that make us social beings in the first place.

A cautionary viewpoint would be that if you aren't part of these new revolutions in social communication, you run the risk of becoming irrelevant to your market. Whether or not your company dives into the fray, social networking has changed the relationship you have with your customers. They are talking about your products. They are telling others what they think of your products—their personal experiences with them. They are engaging you and others, whether or not you engage them back. Think about folks who complain about a service on Twitter. They are shouting into the twittersphere, referencing a company, and the onus is on the company to respond. How does it look to others who may be following that user if the company doesn't respond? How does it look if they do respond and work to make things right? When you see the latter, what do you think of the company? Chances are, your estimation of the value of that company just went up. Each tweet, post, or comment is an opportunity for a win, to connect, to correct, to be a rock star.

Your Company Is Made Up of People, Just Like Your Customers

The answer to the original question about how you are going to justify a business plan for your communities is that your customers are people and its implications can be reframed into a question for your executives. It's not whether you create a community about your product, because, human nature being what it is, your customers have already formed a community around your product. The question then becomes: How will we engage with that community? And more: Will we provide them a home, or a city, for their community to thrive in? Will we reach out to them where they live in "Facebookland" or "Twitteropolis?" Will we reward them when they contribute to the overall knowledge about our products and they help our other customers? Will we give them a reason to stick by our products even when there are missteps? Will we give them a compelling reason to tell others about our product and services; or, better yet, the people who make up our company?

There are plenty of ways to justify the expenditure, but behind any of those are compelling reasons that won't go away if the executives say no to this round of funding. Your customers will still express how they feel about your products. It's up to your company whether you will participate or not. Connecting with your customers by these means may mean customers for life. Ignoring them may have more dire consequences, from public relations disasters to loss of revenue or worse.

Summary

How do you justify expenditure on online product communities?

- Return on investment
- Competition
- Innovation

Humans have always been defined by their social and communicative nature. The very essence that sets us apart from other social animals defines the structures of communities and associations that define our lives, from family, school, and occupation to informal associations like the community of people who run marathons.

These qualities have been explored and defined over the years by philosophers and sociologists, keying in on specific ways to define how we relate to groups. Recently, neurobiology has been turning its gaze toward what makes people so involved in social networks and connected to each other through new forms of communication.

The neurotransmitters dopamine and oxytocin have been found to play a role in driving people to use social media. Dopamine chemically rewards users who disclose information about themselves and who seek out new content from others. Oxytocin reinforces social bonds; when people use social networks online they gain more trust with others using the same networks.

The impact of understanding how people are hardwired to drive social communication about your business gives you insight into why any of the justifications for creating and maintaining an online product community are important. By understanding the user's motivation you can key in on the right metrics to judge return on investment. Understanding the tendency for people to gather into groups around a cause can help you create more loyal customers. By staying on the cutting edge of new technologies, you satisfy the communicative and seeking behavior in your customers and engage your customers in the conversation that is already happening about your products. By listening and watching your customers and employees, you can innovate more quickly—turning tacit knowledge into products and services more quickly than your competitors.

We explore some of these ideas in full later in the book as well as walk through some of the practical decisions you will need to make to create a sustainable thriving community, from defining exactly what you want your community to be to finding the people with the right skills to inspire and drive your communities. We will touch on privacy issues, business impact, and, yes, the analytics you need to measure success. Hopefully you will keep in mind that behind everything we are talking about are people—people who are driven to socialize and communicate, the people who make up your communities.

Community as the Centerpiece for Customer Engagement

Your customers, partners, and prospects are already talking about your product—do you know what they are saying? Are you having a two-way conversation, or are the communication channels one-way? The real question is: Are you engaging your customers?

Many of the traditional marketing and sales activities—such as informing customers about industry trends, making sure they know about your product, providing information during the sales cycle, and helping customers justify the purchase of your product or solution—are all one-way communications. What has changed?

Social media has arrived on the scene! The proliferation of social media has changed your relationship with customers and it will impact your business. The customer is no longer an entity to market your brand and push information. Your customer now owns your brand. The power dynamic has shifted, and customers are communicating to each other and to the company in ways outside of any company's control.

Customers now expect to find information quickly in a self-help mode, including reviews of products from people other than the company's employees. They also expect the option of asking questions of several people and telling others what they think of your products. Communities of people with similar interests among your current, potential, and lost customers already exist. How you engage them will have a huge impact on your business and how your brand is perceived. Customers engaged in conversations about your products are more likely to provide higher customer satisfaction scores, to serve as references, and to have a commitment to your product, which validates your brand. Likewise, the loud voice of a customer in the social world can hurt your business when product quality issues are raised and your organization does not respond in a timely manner or does not meet your customer's needs. Online communities enable organizations to aggregate, influence, and participate in these conversations and are therefore critical for any business operating in today's environment.

Communities in general are created to help people of similar interests and needs connect with each other. They can play a major role in the success of your organization in keeping customers, partners, and employees engaged with your products and services. Regardless of the magnitude of your organization's revenue, work force, geographic distribution, or corporate history, communities can have an impact on your business. If you are a startup company, you might think that you do not need a community until you get a lot of customers. In reality, a community can serve as an extension of your company's marketing resources or as a precursor to your support organization and a key to your future success. The audience you intend to serve will dictate the type of community you build, and in turn that community can help to define what products will succeed.

This book focuses on one type of community: the business-to-business (B2B) community. In B2B interactions, a business sells a product or service to another business. Many of the concepts that we develop in this book apply to business-to-consumer (B2C) as well as B2B communities, but after a brief comparison the scope of this work is confined to B2B.

It is very likely that you have participated in a B2C community. A light starts flashing on your printer, but the printer does not tell you what might be wrong. What do you do? You enter a question into the Google search bar and then review the possible solutions documented by the printer product community. After you try them, you can update the community with a description of your problem and how the suggested solutions worked.

You have just participated in a B2C community. Think about all of the communities you have "subscribed" to by participating in community comment or conversation. These communities might include your favorite hotel or airline, a forum you contacted regarding a product you purchased, or even a program you paid for such as Weight Watchers.

B2B communities consist of employees from the vendor and client businesses. Getting to know the individual participants and developing trusting relationships with those who use their product or services is an important focus for organizations developing B2B communities. For many B2C communities, on the other hand, the primary focus is on understanding and soliciting customers from a marketing perspective. A related contrast is that a B2B community focuses on sharing business expertise and recognizing the experts, whereas a B2C community focuses on consumer opinion of a business's products and services.

To sustain themselves, B2B communities need to solve real business problems, which will vary based on the purpose of the community. As an example, in the B2B manufacturing industry, communities are sometimes used to co-create manufacturing models, with participants from many different companies bringing their best resources together to solve the problem. To be successful, this community would require participants to get to know each other so they are comfortable sharing ideas, expertise, and content. Professional communities, such as those in the medical field, are used to answering questions and sharing expertise. The information must be accurate and timely, and the community members must be extremely trustworthy and credible.

Trust is a key factor that we stress throughout the book. Solving business problems demands that community members trust each other, the content offered, and in some cases the knowledge and expertise of the participants. Building a successful B2B online community takes thoughtful planning, careful decision making, and perseverance. Many factors influence the decisions that will have an impact on your success. Where do you get started? Let's get to work and start your community journey.

Tip   Hold a freewheeling team meeting with white boards and sticky notes to gain a perspective on creating and molding your community.

The X-Factor: What Makes for a Successful Community?

Are you ready for a great deal of work and dedication by your organization? What decisions do you need to consider and why are these decisions important for your success? Just like with any other major program or project, you need to do some planning before you make the decision to create a community and a great deal of work before you launch it. Building a community is building part of your business—you need to make sure you are making the right decisions. In this section, we discuss the fundamental questions that you need to think about for your community, from getting started through implementation.

▇ **Advice** Do not shortcut the process and just start building the technology. Work through the steps and answer the questions we discuss. Otherwise, it would be like building a house without any architectural blueprints.

Step 1: Due Diligence

Before you make the decision to create a new community, you need to do your due diligence. Get into the conference room with your colleagues and really understand why your company needs the community and the value your community members would gain from their participation. What business problems will the communities contribute or help to solve? Are there other external communities that already exist today or other sources of information where your target audience can find the information?

Understanding the business purpose for your community and the value proposition for both the company and the community member are key factors to think through as you consider building a community. Articulating the primary purpose of your community will help you solidify the business outcomes you would like to achieve and lead to a set of defined goals and success measures.

The initial answer to this question of the business purpose of your community may depend on which area of the organization is driving the creation of the community. Each group may in fact have a different starting point, which is fine. You can expand into multiple areas later once your initial community is successful.

Looking from the company perspective:

- If the marketing department is driving the community, the focus could be to gain an understanding about who is influencing the social media conversation or possibly to market and sell more effectively. American Express supports their small businesses with a community. Check out www.openforum.com.

- If the education team is driving the community, the focus may be to help customers get more value from their products and services through certifications and other training, thereby improving customer satisfaction and loyalty. Check out www.cisco.com for their learning network.

- If technical support is driving your community, the focus could be to reduce the cost of technical support by improving self-help and having customers help each other, which would increase the call deflection rate.

This is one of the most popular community focuses. Almost every technology company has a community related to support, such as www.communities.ca.com, www.community.dell.com.

- If the product development group is driving the community, the focus could be to improve the way products and services are enhanced and to acquire innovative ideas through crowd sourcing. Check out SAP's idea place: https://ideaplace.brightidea.com.

- If the product management team is looking for trusted and confidential customer input, your focus could be customer advisory boards. This type of community would be private and accessible only to those who are members of the customer advisory board. CA Technologies uses communities for this purpose.

- If your partner program team is driving the need for the community, the focus could be to bring together support and information for partners. (Partner programs are typically external organizations that work with your company as a partner to deliver sales, services, or support). Check out www.ibm.com/community.

- If executive management is driving the community, the focus could be on visibility and thought leadership by promoting the exploration of concepts and trends to improve your brand and company awareness. Check out http://smartenterpriseexchange.com/groups.

- If a professional services team is driving the community, the focus would be on sharing expertise and experiences and learning from others. Check out www.thepalladiumgroup.com/communities.

How will your community members benefit from joining this community? You will need to answer this question by working through the lenses of the customer. One approach would be to conduct a market analysis to determine what would be valuable to the target audience of your new community. Depending on the purpose of your community, a few examples of why customers participate are:

- Easily find and connect with other customers who use the same products and ask their opinion directly

- Learn best practices and techniques from other customers

- Find answers to questions anytime and anywhere (24 × 7 × 365)

- Gain the opportunity to get to know and interface with company experts and other customer experts

- Provide new ideas and input to product enhancements or even new products

- Co-create a product

- Demonstrate their expertise

- Gain reputation based on expertise from thought leadership to technical guru

Check out what already exists. Search the Web for other relevant communities that may exist on social channels such as LinkedIn, Facebook, or Google Circles. If you find an existing community, determine how active the community is. What additional value can you provide and why would someone switch to your community? Once you can answer these questions, you can start to develop the business plan.

Step 2: Business Planning

Why should your company invest in a community? How can a community impact the success of your business? What are the major goals of your community and how will you measure the initial success? What resources are needed to support your proposal?

A key to the long-term success of your community is to understand how the community goals fit into the larger goals of the company.

■ Tip Take the time to talk with pertinent organizations within your company and help them understand why communities matter and why they should care that the company has a solid, vibrant community. You will need their support in the long term, so start now by getting them involved and garnering their support.

Because every company defines its goals in its own nomenclature, you will need to determine how the proposed community best supports your company business goals.

Communities can help support your goals. A few examples are given in Table 2-1.

Table 2-1. How Communities Can Promote Goals

Goal	Community Business Impact
Accelerate growth.	**Impact revenue growth.** Engaged community members are potential influencers for new sales within their company or recommenders to other potential customers. When customers are involved in the development of a product they are more likely to move to new releases sooner.
Delight customers.	**Improve customer satisfaction and loyalty.** Ability to find answers quickly in a self-service mode, collaboration with other members, and sharing of knowledge and expertise help to improve customer satisfaction. Reduce cost—improved content and self-service tools will decrease the number of support calls and enable customers to find what they need easily.
Be a thought leader.	**Improve product quality.** Pay attention to what community members are asking in the communities to determine what can be improved. Community members have the ability to get involved with product development, from ideation to continuous feedback throughout the produce lifecycle.

Based on your due diligence and the purpose of your community, you will need to write down the initial goals and the benefits of your community. What do you expect to achieve? How will you measure results? And in what timeframe do you expect to achieve your goals? Setting the proper timeframe expectations for achievement of the goals is important because it will take a while to develop a vibrant community. In Chapter 8, we discuss in more detail several ways to measure community business returns and set timeframe expectations.

Tip Start with simple and measurable. You can expand and enhance your community goals over time.

Before you can go to the boss and say that you are ready to make a decision on building a community, there are a few more things you need to consider.

- Be able to articulate in general who is your target audience.

- Validate your plans with a few potential community members. Based on the purpose of your community, conduct a few customer interviews to make sure that you are in line with their needs. You should identify a few proactive advocates who value the development of your community. This group of proponents will be helpful in making your decision as well as in the initial start of your community.

- Define the basic community model—will your community be public, private, or a hybrid? What is the financial model for your community—how will your community be funded? More details can be found regarding these topics in Chapter 3 ("Community Models").

- Define the resources needed to support the community. Who is available today to help and what can you afford in the near term future? You should consider researching case studies of existing communities and finding external research to support your plans. Details on organizational needs and community management are discussed further in Chapter 5 ("Community Management").

- As for any other business plan, write a vision statement.

You are ready to make the decision on your community—align your supporters and present your community proposal.

Step 3: Make the Decision: Yes or No—Should We Take the Plunge?

If your ducks are in a row, the decision should be easy—*yes*. If you are not ready to proceed and there are still a lot of unanswered questions, work through the details until you are ready.

If you do not have support from within the company or your existing customer base to sustain the community, consider the decision to be *no*. The purpose, business plan, and the passion for your community should all be aligned before you proceed (Figure 2-1).

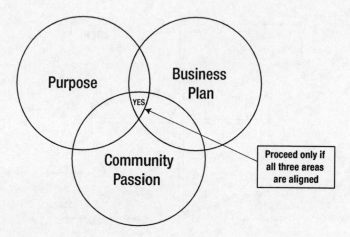

Figure 2-1. Decision-to-proceed alignment

▓ **Tip** Before you commit to creating the B2B community, remember one thing: It is a journey, not a destination. Regardless of how well you create the initial community, you will need to nurture and sustain it. If the interaction and value of the community are not sustained, the community will wither and die.

Step 4: Community Planning

It is time to start laying out the details for your community. Vanessa DiMauro, a leading expert on B2B communities, states: "The *who* will dictate the *how* and the *why*. This means the needs of your specific audience segment or segments will dictate the *how* or type of interactions they will have, and the why encompasses the reasons they participate in your community."[1] (See Figure 2-2.) This premise is the basis for many of the questions we address during the planning phase.

---

[1]DiMauro, Vanessa. *How to Build an Online Community.* LeaderNetworks, Blog, November 16, 2010.

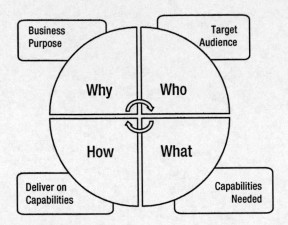

Figure 2-2. Strategy decisions to consider

In your business plan, you have already addressed the business purpose of your community, answering the why question, so you should understand the primary focus of your community.

Next, the *Who* Question

Who is the target audience? Who would be your ideal members? Consider how you defined the business goals of your community and think about the common interests of your audience. For example, technical support communities will attract existing customers who currently use the company product and are looking for information and answers to technical questions, sharing of implementation methods, or installation best practices. A thought leadership community may attract a more executive-level audience with the focus on bringing ideas to the table for exploration and discussion. Educational communities may attract students who want to share experiences about a specific subject or class.

Profile your target members so you can understand how much it will take to get them engaged in the community. Getting members to join may be easy, but to keep them engaged will be more difficult. The more isolated they are, the more they need to learn. The more free time and the less access to other sources of information they have, the easier it is to get engagement. You do not have any control over their needs, but you can build an environment and program plan based on their profile, For example, if your target members are executives, they have very little time. So more community management is going to be needed to do programming and administrative heavy lifting to get them engaged.

A key message when starting the community is *target a core set of users who have a common interest and who will become your initial advocates.* Make sure the interests of your audience match the plans that you are proposing.

Think of this scenario. You have decided to build a community to support your professional consulting services for implementation of health information management systems. Your initial target audience could be students graduating with a degree in health information or related programs; professionals who work for companies that have health information management products; and current health information professionals, including both employees of your company and external consultants. What your target audience would probably not be are general services professionals, other healthcare professionals not working in any way with medical records, or students in unrelated fields. Why? When the audience of your initial community does not have a solid base of common interests, the conversation can become too general and the community inter- action and expertise exchange are diminished. What will happen? Your commu- nity activity will not yield the interaction and expertise exchange across such a broad spectrum of interests and it could wither and die. This is especially true in a new community. You will need your core set of advocates to be the building blocks of your conversation and content, so you need a group of people who have a level of expertise and common interests to be successful.

A few additional factors need to be considered if you are starting a global community that spans across several multicultural areas. You will need to understand if your audience has any potential *language barriers* and *cultural differences.* Language is covered later when considerations for capabilities are discussed. Cultural needs will require more than a translator capability. If your audience consists of multicultural groups, having a local advocate from the region to help set the example would be helpful. You may want to schedule a focus group with potential members to understand their needs and how they would use the community so you can accommodate their needs and gain their trust and buy-in before you launch the community.

TRANSITIONING TO ONLINE COMMUNITIES AT CA TECHNOLOGIES

At CA Technologies, one of the challenges to create our online communities was that customer communities had existed for a long time, some for more than 30 years. Our original "communities" were made up of people who had been meeting face to face on a regular basis, organized by product and regional locations around the world called user groups. In developing our online communities, we brought together the membership from the previous local groups into several global online groups. Over time, we developed new communities for products that we acquired or developed.

Our initial focus of the communities was technical support. The target audience was existing customers who purchased one of our many software products. Our software products span many diverse types of solutions and our customers wanted to interact with customers who had the same products as they did, so separate online communities were created to accommodate the needs and wishes of our community members.

Today, we still have regional user groups who meet in person on a regular basis. These groups are considered a subset of the global community. For many of the original members, the transition to an online community was not easy. Because our online communities were created from existing regional communities, we already had some relationships with community members. However, as we brought together community members from around the world, members needed to develop trust and relationships among a much greater community. Many different groups within our company, such as support, product management, customer success, and community management get to know different community members. We want to know our community members on an individual basis as well as encourage community members to get to know and trust each other, including CA Technologies employees. We also want them to trust the information contained in the community site. Last, we want members to contribute their knowledge to help each other answer questions and share knowledge. The success of our communities is built on participation both from our employees and our customers in a trusting environment.

Tip   Remember, as you start, do not try to be everything to everyone. You will not meet the needs of your audience.

In determining who should be your core set of users to start and who you would want to join and participate in your community, you need to understand their *needs, skills, what makes them tick, and their comfort level to actively participate.* You may want to conduct an informal assessment with your target audience to make sure they are able and willing to participate in a way that supports your community goals. A few examples are noted below.

Technical Support Communities: Effective technical communities share their expertise by providing answers to questions and sharing best practices to help deflect support calls, thereby reducing costs. In addition to reducing costs, many of these community members become your best trusted product advocates.

- Find a few of your current technical customers who are technically credible and whom you trust and ask them if they are willing to actively participate. If your audience does not have the level of experience or expertise to provide value for your community members, you may not be successful; so do not proceed without a baseline of experts.

- Solicit support from a core group of expert employees who will consider participation in the communities as part of their job.

Innovation-focused communities: For communities in which innovation is a primary focus, you need to find community members who are willing to voice their ideas in an open forum. You will also need your community audience to interact on the ideas and be willing to voice their opinion, collaborate, and vote on ideas.

- Talk with a few of your selected core users and ask them about their views on public ideation. You will need a few advocates to seed the process. If you do not have anyone willing to use this capability, then you will need to reconsider your goals and find some advocates who are willing to get started.

- Once your community is active, getting community members engaged in voting on ideas and eventually creating new ideas may be as simple as providing a few examples and education on the process. One caution for ideation: If you collect ideas from community members, someone needs to respond with the actions generated from the ideas or they will start to diminish. The inability to act on these ideas is a major inhibitor to the success of this type of community.

Professional communities: Communities such as specialized consultants, lawyers, or physicians will require a much greater sense of trust and potentially a private or restricted environment. Community models are discussed in Chapter 3.

- You will need to understand the audience needs for privacy and possibly a way to validate professional credentials.

- As you think of your core users, it may be easiest to start with a group of people who personally know each other so that the trust factor exists at the beginning.

- You may want to consider partnering with one of the professional associations to gain your core group of community members or sponsor a third-party community facilitated by a professional association.

Strategy/thought leadership communities: Communities where the members are sharing their business strategies and thought leadership expertise can be similar to the professional community but may not include the requirement of a professional credential. In some cases, thought leadership communities exist for corporate promotional purposes and for the community members to be recognized for their knowledge among peers and others interested in the topic. Other thought leadership communities will be more of a closed community for trusted members to share strategy and help each other in developing new strategies. You will need to assess the needs of your community in order to start your group of core users.

- Find your experts on the topic and see if they are willing to get the community started and maintain a continued level of support. You may ask them to tap their circle of colleagues to join the conversation so that there is some level of interaction.

- A thought leadership community may be more difficult to sustain, so you need to make sure you have the right audience to start, a plan to acquire new members, and a plan to keep it moving. This type of community is more about futures, so the immediate need to interact with the community may not exist. Because executives are busy, you may need a more structured plan such as a topic of the month to get this audience started.

- Communities that focus on areas such as strategic sharing or co-creation will require a tight knit, trusting, and collaborative audience. You will need to find community participants who are willing to share and have a significant level of trust and collaboration. Knowing each other personally in a virtual world may be a requirement to be successful initially in this type of environment.

There is one last thing related to your audience: *social maturity*. Social maturity relates to how familiar and willing your audience is to participate in a social manner using open forums to share knowledge and expertise. You will need a certain number of active contributors for your community to be successful. Even the members who are only consumers of the community information will still need to be willing to check social media channels. Understanding the social maturity of your audience will impact the capabilities you need to deliver.

In the case of CA Technologies, many of our longstanding community members, who were the basis for online communities, were mainframe technology experts whose social media maturity may not always be at the same level as that of some of our new technology users. To accommodate this audience, we added an e-mail feature so they could progressively become more comfortable in the newer online community forum world. We have made significant progress, but it has taken time.

CA TECHNOLOGIES COMMUNITY INTERFACES STUDY

Based on a research survey of CA Technologies community members conducted in 2010 by the University of Toronto, many of the mainframe community members were more comfortable with e-mail and ListServe type technologies than they were with newer interfaces such as Facebook.[2] The conceptual framework developed as part of this project can be found in the summary section of this chapter.

Now to Answer the *What* Question

Now that you understand the factors related to the *why* and the *who*, you need to explore the *what* and the *how*.

You can get individuals to join a community, but what is needed to keep them coming back? You must have a compelling reason not only to join, but also to actively *participate*. This requires that your community finds *value* in participating, value in the content and the capabilities needed to satisfy their needs.

Often, people join a community to be part of the group without understanding what it takes to participate and what value they will receive from it. It is human nature to want to interact with people of like interests, so what helps a person to understand if this community is a fit for them? To feel an attachment to the community, the members must have an affinity with the purpose, the people, or the types of interaction provided. Have you ever joined a community and then discovered there was not a lot of interaction or valuable information? Did you return?

As you start to address what you need to provide, understand the basic *capabilities and programs* that you will offer your members based on your answers to the *who* question. Remember, you can expand features over time.

The capabilities that you chose to initiate with your community will vary based on the needs of the community and the propensity of your community members to engage in each of these areas. Some standard community components include:

> *Message boards*: a message board is an online discussion where your community members can conduct a two-way conversation that is typically available to the entire community. One community member posts a message—it could be asking a question, describing their situation, asking for an opinion of the group, providing best practices, or

---

[2]Lyons, Kelly, Chuang, Steven, and Choo, Chen-Wei. *"Towards a Maturity Model for Social Media Enabled Online Communities: A Case of an Enterprise B2B Online Community."* ACM Digital Library. Available at: http://dl.acm.org/

giving suggested tips. Messages are not real-time conversations such as one would experience in a chat room.

Blogs: A blog typically represents the writer's opinion on a specific topic. Readers of the blog can often vote, like, or comment on the blog. Blogs are typically arranged in reverse chronological order, displaying the most recent blog post first.

Wikis: A wiki is used to allow community members to contribute a large volume of content to a specific topic. Authorized users can add, modify, or delete its content via a Web browser.

Ideation: Ideation is a form of crowd-sourcing that enables community members to submit ideas in a form in which other members can comment and vote. Ideas often relate to new features, new products, new services, or enhancements to existing products.

Document libraries: A document library provides a place where information such as presentations, notes, and other reference information can be uploaded and shared among the community members.

Video libraries: A video library provides a location where community members can access audio-visual components such as YouTube or education videos.

Webcasts/podcasts: A webcast is a recorded meeting or presentation session often held to enable community members to find out information and participate in a live question-and-answer capability. Typically, the webcasts are scheduled in advance on specific topics.

Chat: Chat enables an online messaging capability between community members.

Social channel integration: Social channels are groups such as Facebook, LinkedIn, and Google Circles where community members may also connect with each other. The capability is to enable your community members to link to other social channels directly from another community.

Code sharing: When your community is focused on a technology solution, there may be a desire for community members to share code with the community.

■ **Tip**   When offering code-sharing capabilities, make sure you have the proper legal disclaimer with no liability for the content.

Every audience may not use every type of capability. As you begin, consider which capabilities will provide the most value to your audience and start with a few capabilities that your community can sustain. Table 2-2 provides a few ideas on what may be the applicable capabilities based on the purpose of the community.

Table 2-2. Community Capabilities by Purpose

Purpose of Community	Message Forums	Blogs	Wiki	Document Libraries	Ideation	Webcasts or Podcasts	Chat	Social Channel Integration	Code Sharing
Marketing								Y	
Lead Gen						Y		Y	
Customer Advisory Boards	Y			Y	Y				
Technical Support	Y		Y	Y			Y		Y
Innovation		Y			Y				Y
Knowledge Sharing	Y	Y	Y	Y		Y			
Thought Leadership		Y				Y		Y	

Each capability area just discussed contains "content," or information that is consumed by the community. As you develop your capability needs there are other considerations relevant to the type of content, your company policy, and the needs of the community. The answers to these questions will also have an impact on the community model that you choose. For example, if your information needs to be tightly protected and not searchable for general consumption, you may need to consider a private or restricted model in which the community is not open for anyone to join. See Chapter 3 for more details.

A few content considerations that could have an impact on community capabilities are:

- What is your corporate culture in terms of transparency?

  For many organizations, the culture of transparency is changing to a more open policy with advancements in social media and the increased use of online communities. Today, IBM posts user manuals and documentation in an open searchable capability, allowing anyone access to the information. If your corporate information policy or legal department restricts public access to information such as user manuals, documentation, and other relevant corporate information applicable to the community, you will need to understand how this information will be protected so it is visible only by those who are authorized.

  Another viewpoint for the transparency culture is competitive advantage. Is your company okay with competitors joining your community and having access to the information shared within the community as well as suggested ideas? There are many differing views on this topic, noting both viewpoints—it is okay for competitors to participate and we need to keep some information out of the community for fear of competitors using it.

- Do you have content that should be accessible only to a select group of members based on their role?

- You may have a situation in which only a subset of community members should have access to certain information. You need to understand how you will enable restricted access and protection of the information. For example, you may have an open community but you want only community members who are partners to have access and see certain information or educational videos.

- Do you have content that should be accessible only to those who have an entitlement or are registered for access?

- You may have certain content that you want only current customers to be able to access, so you would need a way to identify these customers and restrict the access. Another model could be one in which some information requires a community member to pay a fee to get access to more information. Again, you will need a way to enable this capability when designing your community capabilities.

- How will you protect intellectual property? In the B2B world, intellectual property is a big deal. You will need to have the proper disclaimers for your community and make sure that your employees have guidelines for disclosure and that they understand the rules of what to post and what not to post.

- If the focus of your community is co-creation between companies, intellectual property would be a major concern and a required capability from the beginning of your community.

- Do you want a wide audience to be able to find the information in your community easily?

- If you want the information in your community to be widely searchable using common search engines, you will need to consider user generated content tagging capabilities to enable and improve search engine optimization.

In addition to the types of capabilities and content you provide, *ease of use and design* of your community features can also affect who participates. Depending on your audience and their comfort level with social platforms, what you offer, and the design, may require you to start simple. You can adjust the customer experience over time. If your community's social media maturity is very low and the preferred method of communication is e-mail, you will need to consider the features needed to support participation and interaction. If the social media maturity of your audience is high, they will probably expect to have capabilities that enable them see each other's faces and connect with people on a more personal level such as through modifiable profiles. As your community matures, the needs of the community will change. A vibrant community with member engagement will most likely see a shift in balance from mostly organizationally developed content to more member-generated content so you will need to stay in tune with the needs of the community continually to keep momentum moving in the right direction. More details on the technical features are covered in the next section.

Finally, Answering the *How* Question

Now that you understand your answers to the why, who, and what questions, the last section of your planning community phase is to determine the *how* question.

How will you support what is needed to create a successful community, meet the needs of your community members, and achieve your business outcomes? How will you fund the technology and resources? What structures are best for your community to get started?

An online community requires a *technical platform*. A Web page is not a community! Everything we have discussed needs to be taken into consideration: audience needs and skills, capabilities, content, look and feel, and ease of use. What other considerations are needed in making a technology decision? First you need to decide the technology platform of the community. Two primary structures exist: on-domain and off-domain.

In an on-domain structure, the community technology platform is owned by the sponsoring company. It is a hosted site that can either reside onsite at the company site, hosted by a community software vendor or hosted in a cloud. The key to an on-domain structure is that the sponsoring company controls the platform. One major decision is whether to use a proprietary platform such as Jive, Lithium, or Telligent, or to develop your own platform using Web 2.0 capabilities such as Liferay. A sample checklist for researching technology on-domain platforms can be found in the Summary section of this chapter.

In some cases, if your community is small or you cannot afford to have your own platform, some organizations start with an "off-domain" structure using

capabilities such as Facebook or LinkedIn. If you are using an off-domain platform, the capabilities are limited to the features currently provided with limited opportunity to customize. A disadvantage of using an off-domain platform
is that it can be modified by the vendor or even deleted without any control
by your company. The advantage of an off-domain community is speed in getting started because building the community platform yourself will take time,
especially when you start with more advanced features.

■ **Tip**   Your content is not as tightly protected in an off-domain structure as it would be on your own
company domain.

The rubber meets the road when you need to answer the question on how
much financial funding is needed to be successful. There are different types of
revenue models that are discussed in more detail in Chapter 3. A few models
to think about are:

- Business-sponsored communities are funded by the company whose products and services are the primary purpose of the community. Typically, there are no fees to join
  or participate in the community.

- Member-sponsored, fee-based communities are funded
  by the community members through various mechanisms
  such as dues, subscription fees, or event fees. Just because
  the revenue model is member sponsored does not mean
  that the community is not associated with one company.
  In some cases the entire community is self-funded and
  run as a separate member-led entity.

- An example of a third-party sponsorship would be if an
  industry association sponsors the community to bring
  together members of the association. Sometimes, adver-
  tising may also contribute to the revenue stream. There
  may or may not be additional dues to participate or
  sponsored events that support the community.

Funding will be needed for an on-domain platform and the people to run the
community. If you have an on-domain presence, you will need to consider
resources to complete the administration and maintenance of the technology
platform. Your community platform needs to be treated as any other production application.

To sustain a community successfully, you will need some level of moderation,
especially for any type of open forum. Chapter 5 discusses the role of the community manager and the resources needed to run your community successfully.

▓ **Tip** Communities require oversight, but are not "owned" by the organizational unit that created or manages them—the entire organization needs to consider the communities to be part of the fabric of the company.

We have reviewed *the why, who, what,* and *how* questions that need to be answered when planning your community.

Step 5: Opening Activities

Like any other business or product, you need to plan how you will get the word out and let people know about the community and get everything prepared to open it to community. As part of your introduction and promotion of the community, you need to make sure there is enough content to grab the attention of prospective community members so they join, come back, and want to participate and stay connected.

- Test your community platform with real users.

- Reach out to a few key prospective community members who will join the community and help to keep it going initially. You will need to consider employees as well as external members.

- Solicit core users to create some initial content—make sure of your community members so as not to start with an empty community.

- Work with your marketing team to develop a marketing and external communications plan.

- Make sure your executives are aware of your community and plan.

- Develop an internal communications plan for your employees, especially for those who should be contributing.

- Develop a social media plan to help amplify the message of your community.

Step 6: Launching the Community

Be ready—now the real work begins. You may not think so at this point, but launching the community was the easy part—now you need to feed the community and provide value to the members, build momentum, and continuously sustain and move forward to improved participation and value.

- Announcements—you will need to continue announcement and promotion of the community both internally and externally.

- Education for members—hopefully, your community will be easy to use and not require a lot of education. This may be dependent on the social maturity of your audience. You may consider small snippets with examples of using the features.

- Supporting community member questions—you will need to make sure that you have someone on your staff available to answer any general questions about your community.

- Continuous improvement feedback—remember this is a journey, not a destination. Any active community will provide ideas for improvement in many areas. At CA Technologies, we created a separate feedback community where our members can ask questions, submit ideas, and talk about the community features versus the information related to the purpose of the community. You will need to have a process to accommodate your community members.

Step 7: Monitor, Sustain, and Evaluate Success

Remember the question at the beginning of this chapter: Do you know what your customers are saying? Now is when you get to start answering that question! You will need to monitor the community in many areas and put business processes in place to monitor the conversation, analyze the results, and evaluate your success. Each of these topics is discussed in more detail later in this book so here are just a few pointers.

- New members—are you achieving your membership targets?

- Activity—how active are your members? To be successful in the long term, you are looking for activity, not just the number of members. What is your response rate to unanswered questions?

- What people are saying—are you monitoring for negative comments? If you find a negative comment, it is critical that you address the comment rapidly with factual information. You may want to check with your marketing department to see if they are using a social listening tool. If the answer is yes, see if you can get the communities added to their search criteria.

- Are you achieving the results and outcomes you originally planned? Is the community activity generating value?

- Enlist appropriate internal groups to contribute content—this is a big area for some companies. Sustaining vibrant communities will take a village to support, not just a few people who manage the community.

- Measure success and communicate to the company—you may not be asked in the first few months, but before you know it, you will be asked to report your success measurements.

Step 8: Continuous Improvement

On the day you launch your community, you will start the list for continuous improvement. You may already have a list of phase II items. Make sure you have the processes in place to solicit the feedback, prioritize the requests, respond back to the community, develop a roadmap, and secure funding to execute the plans.

■ **Tip** On your community journey, you will need to adjust to the needs of your members, technology advances and changes to your company direction.

Vanessa DiMauro once stated, "Community members come to the community for content and stay for community." As your community matures, the community should be a central location for customer engagement in many areas.

Online Community: The Base for Social Engagement

We now get to the real question: Does your community engage your customer and how can you keep members engaged?

■ **Tip** Customer engagement is a key to successful communities, not just a way to communicate with customers.

Communities enable social engagement with your customers and need to become the centerpiece of your customer engagement. However, your community will most likely not be the only social channel used by everyone. You will need to embrace all social channels and work toward your community becoming a social channel of choice for interaction about your product or services and ways to help amplify your community.

Social media is everywhere today and has become a way of communication. Whether you use Twitter to follow people, organizations, or events; Facebook to communicate with friends, like company pages, or join groups; or LinkedIn as a way to stay connected with business colleagues or industry trends, everyone in the business world touches social media in one form or another.

VISION

At CA Technologies, social engagement is embedded into our vision for the communities.

CA Communities are considered a social channel of choice by our customers for collaboration, peer networking, and conversation.

CA Communities provide an experience our customers cannot live without and our competitors will be hard pressed to follow.

Embracing social channels such as Twitter, Facebook, and LinkedIn within your community is important because they are imbedded in the daily activities of many of your members and everyone tends to communicate using tools that they are more comfortable with using. A few ways to integrate other social channels are:

- *Community member profiles*: If you are using an on-domain platform, make sure your members can provide their other social media information in their user profiles. This will enable community members to connect with each other through additional channels.

- *Community branding and content*: Use other social channels to amplify your community value, events, and content by posting information to other social channels with links pointing members and prospects back to your community for the detailed information.

At CA Technologies, we embrace both methods to integrate with other social media channels. We include social media information in our community profile as well as the capability to have a chat between two community members. Our community managers as well as our social media strategists are active daily on other social channels, posting information about webcasts and other announcements related to our communities.

■ **Tip** If your community does not provide what is needed by your community members, they will go elsewhere to find the interactions they desire.

A new customer joins your community and wants to chat or speak in person with a customer who has similar circumstances. How does he or she get in touch with the person? It depends on the capabilities provided by your community. If your community does not enable direct contact but stores information such as that on LinkedIn, they may privately message the person on that channel and connect with his or her as appropriate. As an extension of your community, other social channels will become part of its ecosystem activity and should be part of measuring the social interaction of your overall community.

■ **Note** The concept of integrating many different social channels to engage customers and extending the reach from your community to other social channels is referred by Chris Brogan as homebases, outposts, and passports. You can find more information about these concepts in many social media online resources.

How you keep your customer engaged has been influenced recently by techniques using what is called "gamification." Gamificaiton is a modern business technique that uses proven techniques from social gaming to measure and influence behavior. These techniques can be applied across virtually every user experience to increase specific behavior and add value to a business such as an increase in user-generated content, social sharing, and recognition of contributors. With the implementation of gamification, community members' motivations are actively reinforced, leading to greater participation and the achievement of certain goals.

At CA Technologies we implemented gamification through a program called the CA Champions Program, which influences behavior but also provides our most active community members recognition of their contributions and expertise. When one of our CA Champions answers a question or posts to the community, other members pay attention! Our program is based solely on intrinsic recognition as the prize.

Influencing your community members to stay engaged will yield more than higher gamification-level achievement. Implementing a gamification tool will require that you carefully design the program to match intrinsic motivators and trigger constructive value-added engagement. Too much gamifying can backfire.

▓ **Tip**   Active community members will gain a relationship with your organization and are more likely to recommend your product or service, thus impacting your potential for revenue growth.

The more engaged a community member is with the company and other community members who use your product or service, the more likely he or she will be a loyal customer. This is a factor of building the relationships with people, with community content providing value to customers to improve customer satisfaction and the members themselves gaining expertise. Work with the organizations in your company that measure customer satisfaction and loyalty to determine how you can measure the impact of your community.

Summary

As you can see, there are numerous factors that need to be considered when starting a new community, and you need to assess all of them when making decisions.

The purpose of your community and the business outcomes desired will help pinpoint your target audience. Your audience's needs and skills will drive the capabilities needed to support your community, which in turn drives what you need to deliver your community and how you deliver it.

If the purpose of your community is not clear and you do not identify with your target audience, then you will not be successful. If your target audience is too broad and the community members do not find value in the information, then your community might wither and die. If your community is public and open to everyone but your content needs to be gated owing to confidentiality concerns, you may not provide the information needed to sustain interest.

If you make the wrong decisions, you need to be willing to terminate a poor community or it will become a graveyard on the Web and reflect poorly on your corporation. Think about how you can improve and try again.

There are many paths to building a successful community. We discuss many more details in this book to help you along your journey.

On-Domain Platform Requirements Checklist

End User Functionality

- Customizable user public profile—customer can control and site admin can determine default template
- Ability to add more widgets and default widgets for the page
- Profile wizard for users to create homepage
- Modules for blogs, wikis, forums
- Admin-controllable community templates
- Language translation capabilities
- Permission levels to create community private vs. public hierarchies
- User rights to create communities
- User ratings of comments and tagging of content throughout the site
- Ranking and reputation engine

Admin Functionality

- User, community, and server activity reporting options
- Analytics reporting options
- Obscenity/language filtering or flagging
- Ability to add as well as broadcast external RSS feeds to community modules

Widget

- Widget library that the site admins can feed widgets into for the users to choose
- Widgets rating
- Tools to create JavaScript-based widgets or Google Gadgets nonprogrammatically
- Widgets are Representational State Transfer (REST) based
- Widgets are interoperable with other platforms
- Library of custom APIs to create widgets or plug-ins
- Library of rich social networking widgets

Hosting Capabilities

- Does the hosting vendor host on its own site?
- Do they have hosting partners?
- Can they host the software at a site of choosing?
- Are their recommended hosting facilities co-located?
- Are they SaaS ready?
- Are their recommended hosting facilities Type II SAS 70 compliant and Tier 1?

Application Integration

- Integration with search engines such as Coveo, FAST, or others using federated search
- Integration with SharePoint (if you want to connect to internal communities)
- Support OpenSocial application programming interfaces (APIs)
- Integrate with Face Book/LinkedIn/Twitter
- Mobile strategy
- Single Sign on integration
- Integration with back-end business apps
- Perceived ability to deliver
- In-house experience with the system

Considerations Summary Chart

You can use the following reference chart to make sure you reviewed all of the major considerations needed to get started and understand why these decisions are important.

Questions

Customer Engagement

- Do you know what your customers are saying?
- Are you having a two-way conversation or monolithic communication channel?
- Does your interaction engage your customers?

Due Diligence

- What business problem will the community contribute or help to solve?

- How will your community members benefit from this community?

- Are there other external communities similar that already exist?

  - If yes, how active is the other community?

  - What additional value can your community provide?

  - Why would someone switch?

Business Planning

- Why should your company invest in a community?

- How can a community impact the success of your business?

- What are the major goals of your community and how will you measure its initial success?

- What resources are needed to support your proposal?

Community Planning

- Who is the target audience?

- Who would be an ideal member?

- Are there language barriers or cultural differences that need to be considered?

- What are the needs and skills of the community to make their participation comfortable?

- What is the social maturity of your typical community member?

- What is needed to keep your community members coming back?

- What capabilities are needed to support the needs of the community?

- What capabilities will provide the most value?

- What considerations need to be addressed regarding content?

  - What is your corporate culture in terms of transparency?

  - Do you have content that should be accessible only to a select group of members based on their role?

  - Do you have content that should be accessible only to those who have an entitlement or are registered for access?

  - How will you protect intellectual property?

- What is needed to ensure ease of use?

- How will you fund the technology needed to support the needs of your community?

- What structure is best for your community?

- How will you fund the resources needed to support the community?

Pre-Launch Activities

- How will you get the word out about the community?
- What do you need to complete prior to launching the community?

Launching the Community

- How will you build membership and momentum?
- How will you sustain participation and activity?

Monitor, Sustain, and Evaluate

- What are you customers saying?
- Are you achieving your membership targets?
- How active are your members?
- Do you have the right people in the company engaged in the community?

Continuous Improvement

- Do you have the process in place to collect feedback?
- Do you have a roadmap?
- What funding is needed to continue?

Community Models

Your journey continues as you review your notes on the whiteboard and sticky notes around the room regarding your target audience, business purpose, community interests, and information needed by the community. Now that you have finished answering the planning questions discussed in Chapter 2, you are ready to determine the appropriate foundational models needed to support your community. There are so many pathways, options, and choices that zeroing in on your targeted sweet spot can be more daunting than buying a new car, home, or boat.

■ **Tip**   You should always remain cognizant of the fact that failure is always an option, but it's equally important to remember that "fail early, fail often" is a central part of the iterative process of community and innovation in general. Staying "gumby" (flexible) and being able to "call an audible" (adjust rapidly to unexpected obstacles) are sought-after attributes for community managers and executives overseeing communities.

Proper prior planning can help reduce the number of iterative cycles it takes to gain traction and start seeing measures of success against your business and strategic goals.

So now you are moving to the point where you will have to decide on the foundational structures informing the access and privacy guidelines needed for community members and content, who governs the community, and how the community is financially supported. The structure is a reflection of the decisions you have been making during your initial planning. *Measure twice, cut once* is a maxim in home construction to avoid wasting time or resources on correcting previous missteps. The maxim holds true now that you are building the foundation for your community home.

We're going to examine three areas of community structure: privacy models, governance models, and finance models. Each of these areas has several options or subtypes associated with it. The three areas are not necessarily independent; the choice you make for one area may affect your decisions for the others.

Showing Your Cards: Which Privacy Model Is Right for Your Community?

Privacy models refer the level of restricted access to the information exchanged within the community as well as how selective or restricted the membership will be within the community. Different groups use various terms to describe the potential community models. The premise of the community models used in this book is based primarily on the research of Vanessa DiMauro, CEO of Leader Networks, who describes the three types of community models as public, private or hybrid.[1]

Figure 3-1 shows the relationship of the access levels to the types of community privacy models.

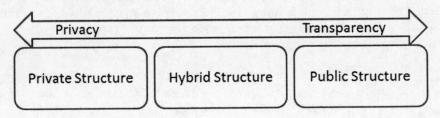

Figure 3-1. Privacy-to-transparency range across privacy models

Public Communities

A *public community* means exactly that—it is open to the public. The members can be all who would like to join the community with the intent of acquiring or providing information on a particular subject. You may already belong to a public community when using social channels such as LinkedIn, Twitter, Facebook,

[1]www.leadernetworks.com/2012/01/11/online-community-decision-public-private-or-hybrid/

Google+ or others. Public communities can also be hosted by your company via a software-as-a-service (SaaS) site or dedicated on-premise environment.

Because the public community is open to everyone, logging into the community site may not be required, although it is desirable for members to be recognized for networking and customer relationship management (CRM) purposes. However, providing access and making information available to anonymous users who are not logged in drives wider consumption of content (albeit not interaction) and draw members and potential members to your site.

Owing to the inherent nature of a public community ("share often, share all"), its primary focus is to make relevant information easy to find through search engines and the community structure/navigation. Therefore, search engine optimization (SEO) is one consideration to be taken into account to ensure your site is found and your information can be found through public search engines or your own federated search capabilities.

Many customers would prefer to find the information themselves by search (or through simple navigation), particularly when the community purpose is to provide self-service help. For many members, finding answers through search or asking a question to the larger community rather than having to pick up the phone and call the help line saves them time. For many companies, providing a mechanism for customers to find information easily—such as the answers to "how to" questions in a self-service model—will reduce the number of calls and thereby their costs. One of our executives calls this goal, "Stop the phones from ringing." When you are able to provide information through collaboration and crowdsourcing and customers stop calling support centers to open support issues, it can quickly contribute savings to the bottom line, and improved customer experience for those who would rather not call in to a support center and just google it.

Public communities can be large or small and both can be impactful and provide value. The value received from the community will depend on the topic and ultimately the vibrancy of the community. However, some people suppose that the size of the network equals the value of the network. That is, a community with an extremely large membership would be an extremely valuable community, because the reach is to a greater number of members.

Small communities may not have a large reach but can be extremely impactful and successful, especially when there is a strong passion around a topic that keeps the interaction alive. This dynamic was explored by Rod Beckstrom of ICANN, who posited that the interaction among the members provides the ultimate measure of economic value.[2] Neither the number of members nor the interaction of members is a completely agreed-upon measure of value, and

---

[2] www.slideshare.net/RodBeckstrom/beckstroms-law-the-economics-of-networks-icann

the debate continues today. Ultimately, the value of the community is determined by the progress in achieving the outlined business objectives. Simple, measurable goals that align with the purpose and reason for being will show the value of your investment. Another consideration that has implications based on the size of the community is the behavior change that the community can influence. Bigger communities typically can expect less impactful behavior changes, such as search instead of call, but the volume of this action has impact. Smaller communities can more easily influence change, such as the way product innovation occurs while the impact of the change is greater but at a smaller volume. Typically it is very hard to get high-impact behavior change at volume—at least not quickly.

Primary considerations for the capabilities needed to start the community are around collaboration and sharing of information.

Advice   Simplistic and intuitive navigation is paramount to success once you have visitors and members within your domain. One of the more frequent complaints we hear about any community is that navigation is a challenge, so that content is not readily surfaced when and where it makes the most sense.

One key factor in considering a public community is that your organization may require a shift to a culture of transparency and willingness to share information openly. This can sometimes be a considerable hurdle to cross given concerns about intellectual property (IP), confidential information (CI), and personally identifiable information (PII). You will need to consider what your organization's boundaries are for the types of content you will be sharing. Obviously, material under a non-disclosure agreement (NDA) would not be suitable for an open community. The understandable drawback to any benefit offered by transparency of information and content is that your competitors may have access to any information posted. This is a discussion you should have with various groups in your organization—such as legal advisors, product management, or marketing—around the risks and rewards of releasing information and the potential downside of providing competitive intelligence to the outside. A key consideration is to have a realistic view of what is actually sensitive material. In reality, much of the information is probably already known by your competitors.

If you choose a public community model, you should strongly consider providing guidelines to internal teams as to what information is appropriate to post and what is not. Although we all wish common sense could be taken for granted, mistakes can occur and they can occur for a variety of reasons. Organizations engaging in social channels should already have documented social media guidelines and policies that could also apply to the community.

Every employee should know the guidelines and who to call when questions not covered in the material arise—as they inevitably will.

Public communities may require closer monitoring—either manually by employees or by leveraging an automated system such as Radian6—than private or hybrid communities. While there are many reasons to maintain a "social ear" and monitor for any potential issues such as information leaks, these social listening tools are also a potential benefit in assisting the organization move from a reactive posture when something bad happens to a more proactive stance in identifying opportunities, such as knowing when a customer needs help, and taking action.

Public communities can focus around several major areas such as the promotion of thought leadership, support, education, and collaboration. The openness of the communities can create more interaction and enhance trust and affinity with the company, as customers absorb how to connect, learn, and share in a transparent environment.

- *Thought leadership*—marketing efforts for demand and lead generation efforts to establish the company as SMEs in their product space

- *Support*—when issues can be discussed publicly and wider participation is desired

- *Education*—100-level education for products to increase awareness and adoption and establish the company as SMEs on their products

- *Collaboration*—creating economies of scale when seeking discussion-type feedback and possibly even voting on suggestions and ideas for their products; particularly desirable in an agile development environment where cycles occur more quickly than in traditional waterfall processes

Private Communities

A private community may be established when the content requires that only those who are members can view or participate, or for organizations whose cultures do not accept using a public community. Private communities are limited to a select group of people who must log into the community to gain access to any of the posted content. This is often referred to as *gated content*. A private community is often smaller than a public community owing to its selective membership, but that may vary based on the nature and design of the community. A private community often centers on privileged groups of members—such as executives, developers, partners, researchers, and key customers—who share private, proprietary, or confidential information.

Private communities can also be relatively open, or they can be quite exclusive. Sometimes all you need to do is request membership; other times you have to prove your credentials and pay a fee.

Such privileged groups include:

- *Industry-specific groups* whose participants feel comfortable sharing information only among peers—perhaps in the financial industry or federal, state, and local government agencies where security is a key concern.

- *Development communities* where product information is shared only with a non-disclosure agreements in place to ensure confidentiality for any proprietary or confidential information. This is particularly important in a co-development or market research community where innovation in a key element resulting in potential patents or other intellectual property.

- *Support communities* for key customers or for a product or set of products where the interaction would provide information of a competitive nature to others—either to the competing vendors or the customer's competitors.

- *Customer advisory boards* whose participants are specifically asked to participate—and the information shared requires a non-disclosure agreement.

Another benefit of a private community is the potential to build more quickly a level of trust among the members, thanks to the limitation of the community to a smaller number of individuals with similar traits, knowledge, and skills. Trust is enhanced by the easier recognition of the experts (by visibly tracking the participation, contributions, and value derived from others in terms of positive ratings) and the ability to get to know the members better and more quickly in a smaller crowd. Trust enables a more open exchange of detailed and specific information. Because the content is accessible only to those already authorized, concerns about losing competitive advantages may not be as acute to cautious executives. Indeed, because many private communities are not even visible to others outside of the current membership, qualified members might not even know about the community and therefore may need to be actively solicited.

Private communities had several challenges in the early days of online collaboration especially with participation. Some of these challenges still linger today, especially when the target audience is executives who do not participate actively owing to time constraints. Mass adoption of social tools such as Facebook, Twitter, LinkedIn, Google+, and others has changed this (to a degree)—and the use and awareness of social tools continues to grow at a rapid rate. Online communities have grown tremendously in size and interaction across the channels, and their use and value are familiar to a much, much wider audience.

You may ask, "Can the community ever get too large?" The answer is yes. Inherent in the natural life cycle of an expanding community is a fissiparous tendency to spawn smaller, more specialized groups—such as subcategories in message boards and smaller new groups around subtopics within a topic—where people can continue to find value amidst what can become a flood of information. When the larger community starts to splinter, this may lend itself to an increase or rise in the concept of the private community again. We will see many more private communities in the future as technology and participants make the interaction more familiar and easier. The desire for networking, the need for special content, an improved user experience through better technology, and ease of use and access will lead to increased success of the private community.

Support in a private community will require additional features, such as registrations, gated content, and a robust permissions capability that keeps the right members connected with the right content. Much of this is often obtainable out of the box with many community applications. Though the company may invest time and effort in additional features or integrations to implement, it should be remembered that customization can lead to additional challenges with version upgrades.

Hybrid Communities

Not sure which to choose? Do you have business drivers that make you wish you had the openness of a public community yet still allowed for gated areas where more private interaction is possible? The hybrid community may offer the best of both worlds—as you can have both public and private sections within the broader community platform. Hybrid communities can be large with selective gated areas or content items that are limited to a smaller subset of the larger community. For example, you could have general information in the public section of the community, but only existing customers would have access to other sections—it could be any group or subset that has a similar need for privacy as seen in the private community.

Keep in mind that hybrid communities will require different content and may require different messages and several types of member engagement within a single community environment. You'll need more content contributors because you may not be able to repurpose content from your other public sites for the specific needs and purposes of the private areas within your hybrid community.

Owing to the potential complexity of the community structure, you'll need to understand the different communities and the capabilities required to function before making final decisions on technology. You will need strong management tools to maintain separation and distinct operations for each audience type. The complexity of the hybrid community may cost more initially. For larger corporations, where the community needs are diverse, hybrid communities can be beneficial because they can address the needs of many different areas and different teams within a single implementation.

The primary drawback of hybrid communities is the complexity of the structure required to support the experience and access for different community constituencies. Many companies have one major community for all areas, whereas others have individual communities based on products or areas of interest. Again, the technology platform must be available to handle the complexity and maintain control. Excessive customization and complex integrations can often lead to challenges with system maintenance, updates, and further development efforts—as well as challenges with administration. Handling as much as possible out-of-the-box is a desirable solution to avoid these potential issues, but your situation may dictate customization.

At CA Technologies, for example, we offer three types of communities within our platform:

- *Public communities* with open registration and content that is searchable on the Internet. These sites contain a mix of internal and customer-contributed content that is indexed publicly by Google and other search engines. These communities are generally organized around our products and are heavily leveraged for, but not limited to, product updates and support initiatives.

- *Private communities* that are visible only to the members who were specifically invited to join, such as a group of customers who participate in a feedback community for development or key customers for our other strategic initiatives that require non-disclosure agreements. None of this content is externally indexed although it is indexed by the company's federated search and is displayed only to members with the appropriate permissions.

- *Restricted communities* that may be visible on the community directory, but membership must be requested and someone must intervene to determine if the individual is qualified to participate and then approve the request. Only after the request is approved can the member access the content. Several of our restricted communities are used for customer/partner validation during sprints in agile development. As with private communities, none of this content is externally indexed. It is indexed by the company's federated search but is displayed only to members with the appropriate permissions to access the gated content.

Your choice of community type will depend on the purpose of the community and the business goals, as well as the needs of community members. The content on which your members will interact and what controls may be necessary to protect proprietary, confidential, or personally identifiable information will also influence your decision.

The hosting platform, ability to use commercial off-the-shelf systems with out-of-the-box functionality, determining what the acceptable level of manual administration is, and other technical requirements will all play a key role in your planning process.

An area that can impact all community models is the resources needed to manage your communities. How you manage the community can vary based on the model chosen. Dedicated community management can be by special advocates or resources within your community program team. Community managers help to maintain the interaction and keep a "social ear" out for risks or opportunities that may present themselves. This can, however, lead to additional overhead resulting from the need for many community managers, advocates, and other support staff to keep the house in order.

How Will Your Community Be Governed?

There are many models of governance for an online community. The model and style you choose will be influenced by the decisions you have already completed including the purpose of the community, the member profile, and the company culture. In addition, you should reflect on your decision of which privacy structure you are choosing and other factors such as how much direct control you wish to retain, regulatory environment, resourcing and staffing available, and of course your technology choice. A key question is: How much do you wish to drive the direction and growth of the community directly (with respect to governance), and how much do you wish to do the same through influence?

The governance of your community can be the responsibility of your own organization and managed internally, can be run or managed by independent or external advocates, or somewhere in between. For the purpose of this discussion, we refer to the governance models as *internal governance*, *external governance*, and *hybrid governance*.

Internally governed communities hosted in external social channels are almost exclusively managed by internal teams, with perhaps some customer or partner-driven unbranded ("in-the-wild") communities scattered about. By virtue of the nature of the community platform, communities on a hosted social channel tend to operate based on the terms and conditions of the social channels in which they reside without much room for collaborative governance among the community leaders other than some of the finer points of what content may or not be allowed and perhaps some additional guidance on expected behavior. Sometimes the *externally governed communities* which exist in these channels will have little or no governance beyond the channel's published terms and conditions and can be "hive-mind" or "wild-wild-West" environments. While there are many interesting conversations that can take place regarding these channels, their characteristics, and the governance challenges that may exist (or that you may be saved from), we will be focusing primarily on B2B social collaborative online communities (usually internally driven).

The influence of control is a key factor in your selection of the governance model (Figure 3-2). The more control you retain, the more freedom of action or flexibility you have. The more you bring customers, partners, and other external advocates into the mix, the less flexibility you may have to put certain measures into place or the less freedom to act in some situations. A tradeoff for control can be less buy-in and shared value creation with your community, which can result in less advocacy by external members. Less control means the community feels more ownership but you don't get to determine the direction of the conversation to the same degree. Another view is that external advocates can lend quite a bit of credibility to your brand—if your customers speak and act on your behalf, you may just be doing some things right. Or they may just be taking action in certain areas where you have left a void—generally by inaction on your part—creating community interaction in spaces and channels with or without your permission.

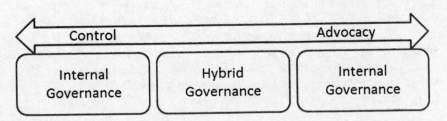

Figure 3-2. Control-to-advocacy range across governance models

Internal Governance

Commonly the organization sponsoring the community controls the privacy model, overall governance and management, financial responsibility for the community, the scope of and reason for the activity, the platform on which interaction takes place, a large portion of the content creation, and maintaining the community throughout the lifecycle. Some of the reasons for keeping the reins and control of the community include:

- Maintaining brand image and providing a consistent experience

- Establishing community for a singular business purpose

- Keeping the content and interaction focused on the desired outcome

- Providing content, interaction, or an experience aimed at a specific persona

Throughout the technology and software industry, many organizations have dedicated communities embedded in their branded online experience for a specific purpose or to address a particular persona. The intent of these organizations may be to establish community interaction:

- Around thought leadership for decision makers and influencers—to position their company and products properly within their industry

- For support purposes to aid in the provision and use of their products within the portfolio—so as to increase speed to return on investment or cost avoidance through call deflection

- To encourage development efforts aimed at crowdsourcing product enhancements and for engaging customers for beta or validation efforts during product development cycles

An important note is that the concept of influence is not absent in this model—you are still seeking to influence the customer/community member; however, more through the positive, organic experience and interaction than external brand advocates. Direct influence with the community may be desirable if your needs dictate that the experience, the content, and the interaction need to be tightly controlled for business process, legal considerations, or other necessary reasons. The internally governed model does not necessarily limit the ability to provide transparency for the organization, nor diminish efforts at establishing trust and confidence, but does so in a controlled environment that can have rock-solid terms and conditions, code of ethics, membership restrictions, and particular rules and guidelines for participation and interaction.

Externally Governed Communities

Giving control of the community to a group of external advocates can be fairly challenging for your organization to accept or manage. There may be an extremely small quotient of control for your organization at times, especially when you need to exert an extremely high level of influence in order to keep the community alive and aligned for the mutual benefit of both parties. There are areas where you can exert influence in an externally governed community such as funding, access to special content, co-branding and marketing efforts, or the ability for the community to drive product direction through direct input.

Tip Beware of communities established by external advocates in an ad hoc fashion through one of the various established social channels or freeware collaborative group/community sites available on the Web. You need to make sure you set guidelines or manage your branded content so you do not find yourself in a situation with old/outdated, incorrect, or self-designed logos, product names, product descriptions, and other misleading content available on other channels. The inaccurate information can be consumed through digital sharing and the pervasiveness of search engines as a primary source for seeking answers and information. Trying to find and just keep track of these communities is a job in itself.

When you relinquish control to external advocates, you need to be aware of potential pitfalls and consider them in your decision. Below are a few considerations that you should think through before finalizing your governance model.

- *The relationship between your organization and the external advocates* needs to be constantly fostered and the parameters examined. When the relationship between both parties begins to deteriorate, the focus could drift from a collaborative nature to one of a more disruptive nature when one side of the partnership line tries to exert their influence through force rather than a mutually arranged and agreed-upon direction. Your organization may be able to try to direct the scope, topics, and activities, but there is very little control unless influence is established and maintained.

- *Protecting your brand* could be a challenge. External advocates may not be able to come close to (or even care about) "staying on brand;" and the interaction within the community, whether positive or negative, may not be associated with your company in many instances.

- *Balance of influence* is a consideration. Without proper governance and moderation, an externally governed community may take on a *hive-mind* mentality. This mentality can take a community founded on a common topic, which has reached such consensus as to be acting as a collective-consciousness entity (everyone has interacted so often on the topic as to be in near complete agreement on a majority of topics—a herd mentality if you will), and leave it to the sway of particularly influential individuals within the community. While not explicitly bad in nature, the switch in influence can lead to challenging situations when the influential individual has an agenda they are able to proffer and drive community actions and statements that may seem "correct" or "popular" at a given time, but then become divisive and contrarian to the collaborative nature of community in the future. Personal gain can be an issue. The influential entity can be an individual or a related or interested group. Perhaps another business such as a partner or a consultancy seeking to establish presence and competing for a marketing or sales advantage within the community—or perhaps to drive the product in a direction that would provide the advantage described earlier. This can be very difficult to identify, challenge, and seek correction for in an open and "less managed, more open" environment where perhaps the members are left to police their own community for infractions or violations of posted policy. Depending on how the hive mind is able to view itself and its actions, it may recognize the derogatory influence and self-correct. However, even if this is identified, it also may not be able to self-correct, and significant action and an extended period of time may be needed to reestablish collaborative efforts and work with your organization to a desired outcome (assuming this is the initial goal of the community).

- This *control of information* challenge exists when inappropriate content is made publicly available. The control of information can be compounded significantly if there are secure and private areas within the community where your organization cannot access information posted and where conversations are taking place beyond the view of those with explicit permissions. In this scenario, you and other interested parties are seeing only a portion of the interaction, not the entire conversation, and there may be discussions that take on a different light or be perceived differently. Though the intent and spirit of the conversations may be positive in nature, obscuring part of the interaction may also reduce trust. In this example, however, you may or may not be allowed to participate in the interaction at all.

At this point, you may have a sour-lemon expression on your face, saying: "This sounds like a nightmare. I never want this to take place around my products or brand. I have to stomp these out of existence immediately!" *Au contraire, mon frère!* Do not fret. The solution is in your approach to community interaction and community management. Please recall some of the recurring phrases in this section and others throughout the book—*openness, transparency, willingness to collaborate, balanced influence, cooperation,* and so on. If both sides approach the activity with these concepts in mind, then having an external governance model could be one of the best possible options—either through the hive mind, through full-on, independently incorporated user associations or communities where there is an independent governing board of officers guiding and directing (and often moderating) the interaction between the community and vendor.

CA Technologies has a long history of working with independent user associations. While there have been challenges for those on both sides of the collaboration line, there has also been great benefit. This benefit comes in a primary form from our perspective—a dedicated board of governing officers, acting as liaisons for the community membership, working for the mutual benefit of the community and our company.

Externally governed models can have officers serve in a multitude of roles, often at low/no cost for their efforts and mostly taking on the role for altruistic/pay-it-forward reasons alone. Some of the roles they may serve in while leading a community are the following:

- Leader
- Advocate
- Arbitrator and/or Enforcer
- Financial Whiz/Magician
- Marketing Expert
- Speaker
- Content Contributor/Curator
- Content Moderator
- Any other hat that may need to be worn for any variety of reasons

The role of advocate has been especially intriguing to us from personal experience, and one that we seek to nurture and develop, For any organization an advocate that is rock solid and even more so for any organization that has any sort of brand challenge in its business lifetime—having external brand advocates of an earned nature is irreplaceable and indispensable. These people have the ability to take your message and carry it to the masses like a megaphone—with the added benefit of having it come from an independent source.

If you are following established and proven principles of community man-agement and acting in a truly transparent and collaborative fashion, external advocates can help your company tremendously by:

- Representing your company and your products in a posi-tive light to members (customers and prospects)

- Providing valuable information from the collective mem-bership based on their interaction and perception with same

- Mitigating any potential flare-ups or challenges in the hive-mind–governed community—acting as advocates and arbitrators to work toward a mutually beneficial out-come in a quicker timeframe

If openness and collaboration through community management are not present, or if they are applied inequitably or infrequently, then the positive results fall short of the mark and the positive message that would have been carried out won't be. Worse, the message may turn toward the negative as trust diminishes and the relationship sours. Influence earned through trust and positive collaboration is a positive benefit when working with commu-nities governed by external advocates or an independent board completely external to your company.

Hybrid Governance Models: The Best of Both Worlds?

The number of possible permutations or business scenarios makes it nearly impossible to describe the hybrid model accurately *en masse*. We think the best way to describe the model is to identify the instrumentality: choosing the best aspects of either externally governed or internally governed models and applying them based on your particular instance, business logic, brand considerations, desired outcomes, and applicable financial or legal concerns or constraints. How that division of responsibility and labor is created and maintained can determine if a community falls within the category of a hybrid governed community.

THE CA TECHNOLOGIES GOVERNANCE STORY

The hybrid model—or, more accurately, the span of hybrid models we work with—is indicative of the overall CA Technologies approach toward communities and community management.

As the community program is one of the longest-standing customer programs at CA Technologies—some of our mainframe communities first incorporated in the early 1980s—there have been a multitude of approaches to and efforts in support of community over the years. Some of our program changes have been driven by the evolution and historical events of the company, and some have been driven by the evolution and revolutionary advance of technology with regard to online collaboration. We'll chat more about some of our program updates in Chapters 4 to 6, but for now we would like to focus on the governance aspect.

In our overall governance model, we have examples of each of the three types of governance models described here:

Externally governed communities. We have a few truly externally governed communities: independent user associations that are incorporated separately from our company and have their own articles and guidelines, but that collaborate with our internal teams in support of the products or interests they represent.

Hybrid governed communities. These are communities for various products where there is an external board to govern the communities along with an internal community manager to help guide the internal interaction and help the board officers. Some communities' memberships cannot identify leaders to act as advocates for the community and assume leadership. By default, these become hybrid communities, as they are governed and managed by our internal community managers until an external leader is named.

Internally governed communities. Our internally governed communities tend to be less product-focused than the other two types and more motivated by business needs. An example of such a community is the MyCA Feedback Community. This is an open community for community members and leaders to collaborate on the community program. It's the platform we use to support community interaction and several other business functions that collaborate with the program, such as our CA Technical Information Team and CA Global Support. Other examples are our development communities that were established to enable customer validation during the agile development process for our products and our CA World community, which includes members who are attending the event. The CA World community provides a place for attendees to find information about the event, have conversations with others attending, or ask questions about the event that are answered by our CA World team at CA Technologies.

The majority of our 40+ product communities are governed by external board officers who are advocates for our products. With such a large number of external community leaders, it can be quite a challenge to balance, maintain, and grow our community leaders to assist in enabling the members and driving community interaction.

In our hybrid model, we work collaboratively with our Board Officers to sustain our communities at the highest possible levels. We provide the primary platform for collaboration, with our legal terms and conditions. We encourage the use of social channel outposts to expand the footprint of our communities, each with their own terms and conditions set by the social channel and then extended by the community moderators. We provide overall guidelines for the CA Community effort. Each community may or may not have their own independent or extension of those overall guidelines.

Though the complexity presents a myriad of challenges on a regular basis, it is well worth the effort and investment. We are a company that has had its share of brand challenges. However, in working to create and enable these groups of community leaders and by investing in the communities, we have seen a significant return with regard to helping improve our brand alongside the efforts of our marketing and other related teams. As depicted in Figure 3-3, we are able to have relatively small and agile teams of community managers and internal entities work through the community leaders to expand their influence and therefore the collaborative and innovative efforts within the communities.

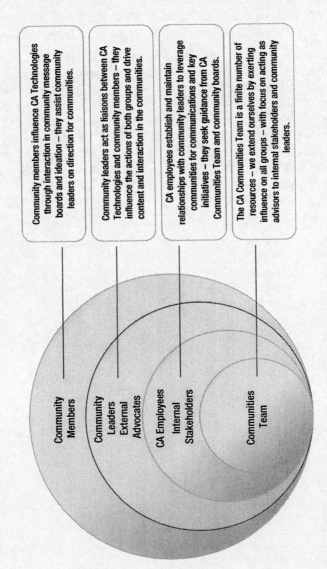

Community members influence CA Technologies through interaction in community message boards and ideation – they assist community leaders on direction for communities.

Community leaders act as liaisons between CA Technologies and community members – they influence the actions of both groups and drive content and interaction in the communities.

CA employees establish and maintain relationships with community leaders to leverage communities for communications and key initiatives – they seek guidance from CA Communities Team and community boards.

The CA Communities Team is a finite number of resources – we extend ourselves by exerting influence on all groups – with focus on acting as advisors to internal stakeholders and community leaders.

Community Members

Community Leaders External Advocates

CA Employees Internal Stakeholders

Communities Team

Figure 3-3. Zones of influence model in CA communities

Whichever governing model you choose, applying the principle of minimal sufficiency with regard to governance is the most likely way to maximize and encourage participation from leaders, members, and colleagues and to allow for widest possible avenue to collaborate and innovate. Just keep a watchful eye and work with all parties (especially perhaps your in-house counsel and other legal and financial expert resources) to protect the company and members. From control to advocacy may seem contradictory, but they are important in equal weight for the community effort overall.

Which Finance Model Is Right for Your Community?

The finance model dictates how the community is funded initially and sustained over time. The model you choose depends on the funding your organization has to invest in the system, the program, and the community management or how much you want for the community to invest in itself. Is your community a fee-based model where the expected outcomes are in created revenue? Or is your expectation cost reduction, such as the example of the self-help support-type community? It's a balance of matching up the desired outcome for the investment in community against the resources available. In this section, we focus on the internally-funded or hybrid model. You probably already surmised that you might not have or need to contribute to a totally independent community. In fact, financial support from your organization may not be desired or sought in the first place. If there is a truly independent community representing your organization whereby your organization incurs little to no expense, the outcome can be a significant return to your organization.

The internally-funded finance model is the easiest and simplest to understand from an external perspective. Generally, it is incumbent on the organization that is sponsoring the community to fund any and all expenses incurred in the support of the community such as the resources applied for interaction either in terms of community management or other teams in support, and for the platform itself. Though internally -funded and driven finance models appear simplistic from an external perspective, anyone who has managed a community, the platform, and related activities knows that the simplicity ends there. Determining how the funding—in terms of the platform, its development, allocating staff for dedicated community management, supplementing content curation, and dedicating staff/resource time to interact with the community—is applied is as complex as your organization determines it needs to be.

The hybrid model is equally complex but may be necessary for a variety of reasons, including:

- To create or fund a platform for online collaboration that the community is not able to fund and which you do not wish for them to leverage as an independent social channel.

- To provide your community leaders and advocates with a measure of autonomy of action with regard to raising awareness (enabling independent marketing) and/or increasing activity within the community via speaker's fees or other incentives for participation.

- To augment dues or funds garnered from other sources.

- To assist with the funding of in-person activity such as events and user group meetings as an extension of the collaborative activity taking place online.

Some questions that you should consider when determining the financial model include the following:

- Who will fund?

- What resources are available such as people to manage the community or systems to support the community?

- What should the mix of investment be between the platform, resources, content, and external expertise?

- What are your measures of success to continue investment?

- How will you determine your return on investment (ROI)?

  - Leads/Referrals

  - Direct and indirect sales

  - Cost avoidance through call deflection

  - Product ideas generated—improvements in development cycles

  - Customer satisfaction and loyalty gains

The answer to the question of which financial model you will choose may be simple or complex depending on if you have the money to spend, or the need to spend it based on the business goals, privacy model, governance model, and the platform necessary to enable the collaboration in online community.

Summary

There are many choices to be made when determining the architectural structure of your community and many decisions you must make in determining which privacy, governance, and financial models are right for your organization. Based on the considerations discussed in this chapter, you will need to take the time to work though answering following questions in order to proceed:

- *Privacy model.* How open can you be with your content and collaboration?

- *Governance model.* How much control do you need to maintain or how much control is given to external advocates?

- *Financial model.* What model is necessary based on your privacy and governance models?

It can be challenging but not impossible to change the type of structures you choose for your model. It pays to not only think about the current needs but work through the vision of what you want it to be five years from now, based on your company's strategy and its path to success.

Life Cycle and Maturity Models for Online Communities

Life cycle. Maturity. Transience is eternal. Cycles of growth and decay are infinitely scalable, and community managers and members see signs of them every day in their online interactions. The concepts are scarcely unique to online communities.

The other day my oldest daughter was asking about the Earth: How old is it? What stage of life is it in? Will it ever end? Pretty deep thoughts for a nine-year-old, but it brought about some interesting conversation around the various cultures and religions in the world. Why do some seem to have stalled at one stage for centuries or even millennia, while others evolve rapidly from stage to stage, die off, or rejuvenate themselves? Given the fairly low short-term probability of an apocalyptic earth-ending event, it appears that most communities in the world will continue on the path of life cycle and maturity.

The conversation got me thinking about the communities I lived in and traveled through in my life. Having grown up in the tri-state area surrounding New York City through the latter part of the 20th century, I saw some of the urban areas starting to decline and many of the outlying areas beginning to flourish as the exodus from the city to the suburbs began. When our family moved from the Bronx to Long Island in the early '70s, we found ourselves surrounded by large expanses of farmland, open fields, and woods. Over time, this space was consumed by residential and commercial growth as the urban areas (which had provided a large part of the population for the suburban boom) started entering a phase of gentrification and economic reinvestment which has brought many of the neighborhoods in decline a new life and an additional stage in the life cycle of a community.

This inevitable aging process is now appearing to take place in the surrounding suburban areas I saw establishing themselves throughout my youth. These communities are now established. Some are mature and the initial signs of decay are apparent. Some communities are proactively working to address the deterioration, but others are locked in a vicious circle of dwindling finances. Many of these communities have dedicated small, local governing entities (incorporated village governments, chambers of commerce, etc.) that work to drive revitalization and upkeep. These leaders measure the health of the community and seek to keep it thriving for the sake of the residents.

I see the change in the housing as homes are rebuilt and restored. Younger people come in and tear up what the previous generations have built through massive home improvement projects that bring neighborhoods up to date. Similar changes in commerce and industry throughout the areas are apparent. Many of the industrial giants that helped the communities establish and grow are now gone, and their buildings and space have been repurposed as we have moved to being a service economy instead of one based on production. I wonder if any of the areas will become like some of the industrial ghost towns one sees in upstate New York and Maine, despite appearing more resilient by virtue of lying in the penumbra of a thriving megacity. Having access to the infrastructure, resources, jobs, and charisma of the metropolis helps surrounding communities maintain their luster and desirability.

I hope by now you are seeing the connection between real-life communities and online communities. Online communities are planned for, grow out, establish themselves, mature, are governed, sometimes die, and yet are often reborn—much as real-life communities have done for thousands of years. We will examine here aspects of the life cycle and maturity of online communities, in much the same way as an anthropologist conducts an ethnographic study. Our culture is conditioned by ever-quickening access to information coupled with near-universal adoption and leverage of social collaborative tools in all spheres of life. In consequence, community life cycles are shortening as their constituent stages are crossed more quickly.

In the next sections, we examine two four-stage models that address different aspects of community life cycle and maturity—one that provides a high-level overview and the possible rejuvenation of an online community, and another that offers additional insights on the progression of the competencies within each stage. Each offers unique perspectives in relation to the life cycle of online communities.

A Four-Stage Community Life Cycle Model

It's easier to look at the elements within the life cycle mapping from a macro level before digging in and examining some of the finer points or micro level perspective. Rob Howard, CTO of Zimbra provides a simple way of categorizing a community into one of four stages: *onboarding, established, mature,* and *mitotic* (Figure 4-1).[1] These categories help determine where along the life cycle path a community may be. From there, you can get more granular in your examination and begin determining what actions are necessary to advance your community to the next level of maturity. It is important to note that some communities may fall in between two of the stages described here as they make the transition from one state to the next.

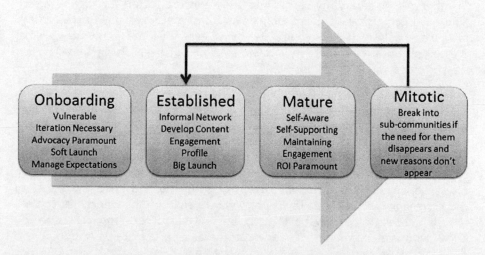

Figure 4-1. A Four-Stage Community Life Cycle Model. (Adapted from Rob Howard, http://mashable.com/2010/07/30/sustainable-online-community/)

Let's examine more closely the stages into which a community may fall.

---

[1] Rob Howard posting on Mashable July 30, 2010. Available at: http://mashable. com/2010/07/30/sustainable-online-community/

Onboarding State

An *onboarding community* is a brand new and forming community, with the membership comprised of your early adopters and other interested parties who want to learn more about what you are doing. In our world, it may be for a new organically developed product, a product that comes in through an acquisition, or a spin-off from a mature community that is experiencing some form of mitosis. At this point, you most likely have a community platform, a limited membership, and are providing the majority of the content. "People come for the content and stay for the community"—sound familiar? This is the point at which you are amassing content of value, and building the sense of community around your product/topic by engaging in the content you are posting.

For an onboarding community, there is quite a bit of iteration as members figure out, and possibly help develop, the rules (governance), the culture, and the value of the community. Keeping an agile mentality and approach is extremely important. Leveraging an entrepreneurial attitude and approach can help significantly: essentially, you are starting up a new business and the members are your customers (both internal employees and external customers or partners should be considered members). A critical part of this is engaging key stakeholders and membership, on a very regular basis, to see if you are getting it right and where you may need to tweak things a bit to make sure you are staying true to the promise to deliver value to your active members. The idea is to create a virtual online collaborative space that is a win–win situation—mutually beneficial for the sponsors and the participants.

This is generally when a community is at its most vulnerable, when it has the greatest chance of failing, and therefore it requires a lot of attention and nurturing by the community manager and the lead advocates/evangelists. There needs to be a high level of engagement by these teams to bring community members into the fold (often holding their hands), describe the different ways to interact with each other, show where the provided content will be displayed, answer any questions that may come up, and raise awareness of the community and celebrate its wins as a way to embrace the theory that success breeds success. You may be directly inviting customers and partners you know who are community-minded to come and participate—developing and cultivating your initial advocates in a planned and calculated manner.

The key to succeed in a new forming community is to keep it simple and make it easy to understand, easy to participate, and easy for the members to recognize and receive value for their time and effort. It's important to recall Metcalfe's law from our discussion on community models: the size of the network does not equal the value of the network. A small community of active members is inherently more valuable than an extremely large network with a relatively low number of active members. Although it is desired to have a large membership eventually, the activity needs to grow proportionally to the membership. It is important to set proper expectations with your stakeholders and executives on membership growth, as this is one of the biggest challenges in community management. It's imperative for everyone to be patient while the membership base develops, for unexpected challenges and issues can arise if membership growth is pushed too fast.

During this state, many community management practitioners advocate for a *soft launch*—starting small and then developing to the point where the community is well enough established to support a *big launch* out to a wider audience. This is one way of ensuring that when larger numbers come in to interact, there is already content for them to engage in and other members to connect and network with. Remember, it's not the system that makes or breaks a community, but the sense of connection around the common topic and associated content that makes it great. An established culture and properly set behavioral expectations allow a community to scale productively.

Celebrate the large number of small wins as a way to demonstrate value to prospective members in advance of their participation to draw them in past the barriers to participation and to overcome other social channels that will compete for their time. Celebrate your advocates; they are your co-founders in this endeavor, so finding ways to recognize them is incredibly important. They will help with new content, answering questions, and promoting your community (and your brand) through word of mouth—a type of promotion that can be much more valuable than paid-for promotion.

It can be very challenging to overcome a first impression, so putting forth your best effort is essential, and an assurance of organic growth on a solid foundation will make a good, long lasting first impression.

Established State

An *established community* is a community that has made it past the start-up phase: the planning, execution, and hard work have paid off! You have grown your community through promotion and search engine optimization, cultivated your advocates and leaders, and by their word of mouth, you have advertised to other customers. At this point you probably still look at your membership metrics, but maybe not as closely and you are now much more focused on engagement tactics and metrics such as participation and value. The effort within your company has also spread from the core team to a wider, more expansive effort across the company.

In an established community, the members have started to create an informal network—with each other, and with subject matter experts within your company. The leadership of the community has created a governance structure that helps promote the reason for the community existing in the first place. If there is a true sense of community, the membership may even take on the role of self-policing and providing guidance in how to interact and engage properly with the members. Content is contributed both by the company and the community members alike, and across a wider spectrum of channels (message boards, webcasts, ideas, wikis, etc.). All of this is apparent in the culture of the community and how the members interact with each other. Something to note here is that it may have taken weeks, months, or even years to reach this point depending on the growth rates of your company, your customer base, and efforts within the community. Having your community grow in a viral fashion can be great, but it is not always the case.

The *90/9/1 rule* traditionally has been seen as a constant in online communities. The rule is that you'll have your hardcore advocates (1%) who seemingly never sleep and take the lead in generating content and answering the questions of your occasional contributors (9%). In watching your analytics, you'll see that the majority (90%) of your community are "lurkers." This is not necessarily a bad thing, although you do want to move them to become more active over time. If you are measuring your view count, you'll see that this part of the membership is still deriving value by consuming the content that lies within the repository you have built jointly with your customers and partners.

Recent research by folks at The Community Roundtable shows that 90/9/1 as the base numbers are not as steady as believed in the past.[2] They show that the average engagement profile for an online community has the vastly different ratio of *55/30/15*. The difference has been attributed to the type of community and applied levels of active community management—in other words, factors that increase engagement skew the rule-of-thumb ratio.

You may have found, as we have, that taking an a la carte approach to the services and content channels you serve can be the way to go. Your community will tell you that bells and whistles are nice, but having the features, functions and content channels, that have proven to be popular among the membership, are where you should focus your time, attention, and efforts. It is good to remain exploratory when new options arise, but continuing to deliver the primary value for your active and engaged membership is paramount. If your webcasts and message boards are where the bulk of your engagement is taking place, and there has been little attention paid to blogs or wikis, this is a good time to find out why, and to determine if blogs will serve a part of the business that will benefit customers as well. Even in an established community, changes in technology and in your business allow for further growth in terms of content.

---

[2]The Community Roundtable. "The 2013 State of Community Management." Available at: http://www.communityroundtable.com/research/the-state-of-community-management/the-state-of-community-management-2013/ (Accessed on July 10, 2013).

This is probably where, now that you have a solid foundation and have built a nice home for your community, you want to go for the big launch. When your community has established itself you will have much more quantitative and qualitative data and examples with which to build your launch material out with and get more value for your efforts and budget as well as increase your return on the investment (ROI). You will have a strong base of community leaders and power users to act as advocates during your launch, providing additional perspective to your messaging and content—something that will most likely be seen as more powerful and more valuable than the company acting and communicating individually. This is one of the milestones you've been working hard for and it is important to celebrate it with your active and engaged members who have been your advocates in building a successful online community. It's just another way to show you appreciate their efforts in helping to expand a fledgling community into an established one and that you still want this community to grow and eventually mature.

Mature State

The ideal mature community is one that has been established for several years and has grown to the point of being relatively or virtually self-sustaining. At this point, the top of the mountain if you will, the community is hopefully seen as a fully meshed network where the engagement between internal teams and members is frequent and the relationship holds a high level of transparency. The internal teams help onboard new members, as do the established membership, and it may even be possible that the members help onboard new employees in a collaborative fashion. The network holds value in terms of the longstanding relationship and the shared knowledge that the internal teams and the membership have jointly created. The passion within the community has led to true collaborative development for the product or aspect of the business you have created the community to address.

The content channels, and the participation within, are well proven and activity occurs on a regular basis. The cadence is also well established, as it has become just a part of doing business with each other. You may or may not have broken free of the 90/9/1 rule but you have definitely increased the numbers within your 1 and 9 percentage groups. By now you have increased your expectations and moved the goal posts several times—further developing your content initiatives and reexamining your metrics and measurements for success. You have taken the content and interaction within the company and developed product and information that helps continue to drive the business—in effect, monetizing the community interaction. These products may be ideas or enhancement requests for the product or perhaps leveraging data mining to deliver critical information to internal teams to facilitate and improve the delivery of support, technical information and documentation, creation and targeting marketing content, adapting service offerings, and so on.

As the business and the technology have changed over the lifespan of the community, your view on community value and ROI have most likely changed and new opportunities (or challenges) have arisen. Membership growth is no longer a primary metric but one used as a base ratio for all of your other metrics and analysis. These metrics and analysis are the basis for your decisions with regard to community management and continuing investment in the community. They are well established and are shared throughout the company, and what is relevant is shared with the membership.

Some of the possible issues that appear here are in keeping the content and interaction fresh and appealing to longstanding and new members alike. It can be a challenge to accomplish this in a manner that keeps the content in line with the consistent theme or topic for which the community was established. It can be a further challenge to manage your advocates—longstanding members who have power and influence. Collaboration is needed with the community managers and content providers to ensure that expectations are properly set and there are not divergent routes to continued community success and evolution.

As you may have noticed, I started this section with the qualified phrase, "The *ideal* mature community…" [emphasis added]. This is the potential state to be achieved if you planned well, executed well, employed proper and solid community management principles and tactics, received customer support and participation, and so on. Sometimes communities need to find a new route—and of course, failure is always an option.

Mitotic State

Sometimes successful communities become so big that they need to split into new groups or find ways to revitalize the interaction to continue succeeding and providing value to the membership. Contrary to Metcalfe's law, sometimes a community may become too big and the content so expansive that subsets of the membership find the need to branch out and create new communities or subsets within a given community to continue receiving value. This process is analogous to the biological process of *mitosis*, by which a mother cell separates into two daughter cells with identical DNA in furtherance of the body's overall growth and development processes.

I don't think we can say it's inevitable, but I would venture that it is preferable to a community dying outright as long as the new venture delivers on the promise of value. Communities can die, though, if the need for them goes away —some topics become irrelevant and products are declared to have reached end of life status. This should not be seen as failure necessarily—as with real-world communities, sometimes things that were once good and great do come to a natural end. The community life cycle is tied to both the product and customer life cycles.

Sometimes the need or desire to interact morphs to a new state—bringing the community back to either the onboarding/formative or mature state. We have seen this happen many times within our mature communities—and there have been several different reasons why it has happened and how. That is, the original problem the community came together to collaborate on may have been resolved or , but more or new problems and challenges may arise.

CA Technologies once had a product that was a suite or collection of options around a central product. There were many regional communities for this collection of products and they were very active in the development and support of it. Over time, the options grew up, and were developed into products of their own and sold individually or grouped into different bundles and/or suites. As such, and along with the fact that a majority of our members identify themselves by the product(s) with which they work, there was less interest in getting together collectively (the original purpose of these communities) because the users of one product were less interested in the other products unless there were integration points. So the groups split and eventually reformed into individual communities that focused on the specific products they were to represent. Each community now has its own identity and culture and has progressed from the formative phase to become established—and some have even progressed to a mature state and may, in time, be seeking ways to revitalize themselves.

Some of our more mature product communities, with a life and history that spans multiple decades, have embraced a shift in and reduction of interest in attending in-person meetings (in what we referred to as regional user groups) and reinvigorated the online interaction by introducing subgroups known as special interest groups (SIGs) within the larger community. They have decided to examine various topic areas that relate to the product as a way to drive new conversation around a product and membership has been around for some time. The community is organized around one of our mainframe database products so they are now fostering interaction around three new areas: Application Development, Database Administration and System Programming, and Management. Breaking down to certain, specific topic areas by adopting a new perspective or viewpoint of an established topic has allowed the community to continue collaborating. It'll be interesting to watch and see if these SIGs become successful enough in their larger community to merit a move toward becoming a community in their own right—something I will be watching for in the future.

Now that we've examined the life cycle of online communities from the macro level, let's dive a bit deeper into the various aspects of maturity that a community will seek to develop as it moves from one stage to another.

An Alternative Four-Stage Community Life Cycle Model

One of the models we often reference when assessing which stage a community is presently at is one developed by the folks who run The Community Roundtable—a community of community practitioners. The model was developed collaboratively between the leadership and the members, and though the stages within the life cycle are termed a bit differently than what we have discussed so far, the principles are primarily the same. The reason why we often reference this model as well is because it offers additional perspective in that this evaluation further breaks down the different stages across eight competencies that they consider essential to the development and success of an online community (Figure 4-2).[3]

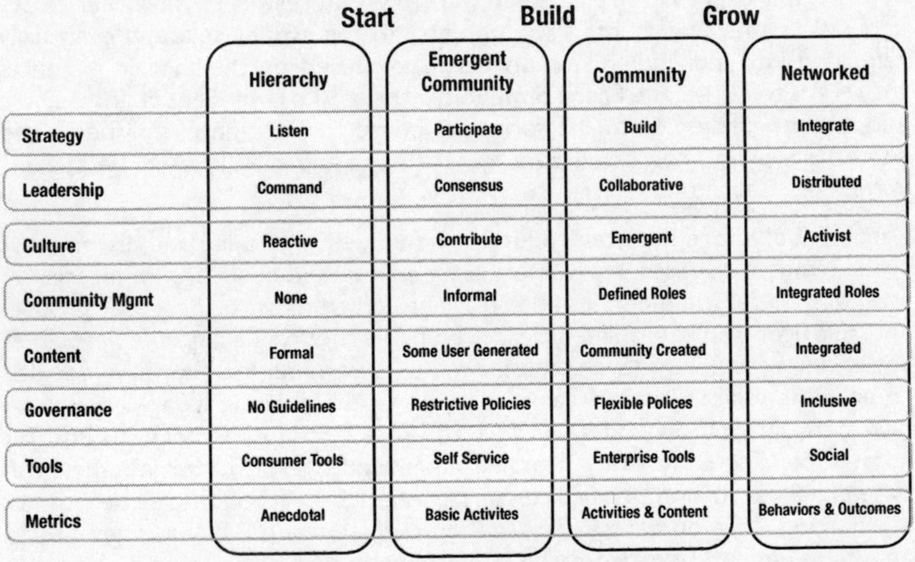

	Start	Build	Grow	
	Hierarchy	**Emergent Community**	**Community**	**Networked**
Strategy	Listen	Participate	Build	Integrate
Leadership	Command	Consensus	Collaborative	Distributed
Culture	Reactive	Contribute	Emergent	Activist
Community Mgmt	None	Informal	Defined Roles	Integrated Roles
Content	Formal	Some User Generated	Community Created	Integrated
Governance	No Guidelines	Restrictive Policies	Flexible Polices	Inclusive
Tools	Consumer Tools	Self Service	Enterprise Tools	Social
Metrics	Anecdotal	Basic Activites	Activities & Content	Behaviors & Outcomes

Figure 4-2. The Community Roundtable Community Maturity Model. (Courtesy of The Community Roundtable)

What we'd like to explore now is why these competencies are important and some considerations about each one to have in mind when planning for or working with your online communities.

---

[3]The Community Roundtable Network, 2009. Available at: http://www.communityroundtable. com/research/community-maturity-model/

Strategy

As the cornerstone of any community, the community strategy should be aligned to the corporate strategy for maximum impact and follow the same iterations in planning and execution. As the community matures, so should the strategy designed to drive it to the next level of maturity. There will be an initial strategy but, over time and in conjunction with your advocates and key stakeholders, your strategy should continue to be built upon because as your community matures, so will its ability to add complexity to the strategic planning and execution necessary for continuing growth and success. While an early approach to strategy might be simply to provide content and interact on it, at some point it may develop and be ready to be integrated into every aspect of how the customer and company conduct business—purchasing, implementing, supporting, developing, and other activities along the product life cycle.

Leadership

Leadership can be a difficult area of progress along the maturity path. Irrespective of whether leadership is internally based, externally based, or a hybrid in-between, changes in people's lives and careers can make maturation a long and challenging process—especially when you are collaborating with people who have other primary jobs, active family lives, and other entities that compete for their time, whether they are internal executives or external advocate leaders.

Company executive opinion should evolve from a perfunctory acknowledgment that community is a nice thing to have to a firm understanding that community is essential inasmuch as it confers customer loyalty, support, and other benefits. The maturation that takes place here is in understanding how community interaction directly impacts both the top and bottom lines of the business. This progression can be challenging because it takes proper setting of expectations and thorough development of metrics and analytics to show the level of impact and how efforts and investments create ROI for the overall community investment.

It's also important to recognize that activists and content contributors may be key members within the community, but a content contributor is not always a leader at heart. Despite the inherent challenges, it is extremely important to have leaders to guide the communities as they set the tone for the culture and enforce the governance that keeps the community growing and moving along, particularly in the early stages of a community life cycle. Over time, as the culture becomes ingrained and the community super-users learn how to self-police and keep order in a community, the leadership can become shared, and, as the diagram indicates, transition to a distributed model that can extend leadership to varying levels through larger and more complex communities. In the military, they use something understood as the Commander's Intent (CI) to achieve order and understanding while engaged in operations. The CI explains the purpose for the action, the desired end state, and any key tasks or milestones along the path to the desired end state. This allows subordinate leaders, although still placed within a hierarchy, to lead and achieve in the absence of direct communication from higher authority. Instead of directly leading, the leaders of a given community can lead more by influence than by direction with this model.

Culture

Culture can be viewed as a thermometer within a community. In the early stages of a community, the culture may change as the community grows—and the culture is a good indicator of how healthy the community may be. A collaborative, transparent, and happy culture is obviously what is desired—but the inevitable challenges that will arise in any community, be they around leadership, governance, difficulties in collaboration, and the sharing of information can weaken and damage a positive culture, create both obvious and hidden barriers, and turn things a bit sour. This sourness can become a malignancy and irreparably damage a community, or it can be addressed through engaging leadership, community management, and open and honest communication to address whatever concerns are causing the cultural rift. Understanding cultural limitations of both the organization and the community is important to establishing operating guidelines that keep all parties that participate in the community happy, productive, and engaged. Eventually, what you want with regard to maturation of your culture is for it to turn from the thermometer that can be an indicator of the health of your community into the thermostat that controls the health of your community. A healthy, positive culture will energize your community and make it resilient to challenges, issues, and possible troublemakers who can inhabit a community and try to turn the heat up unnecessarily.

Community Management

As discussed in Chapter 5 in greater detail, online community management is a relatively nascent role and is a mix of art and science in its theory and application. Before a community is launched, the community manager is acting in an advisory capacity—planning the strategy and initial execution for the community. In early stage communities, this tends to change and the role can become largely administrative and often feels like you are pushing a boulder up a never-ending hill. This work is important and necessary—and poises the community to continue growing and flourishing. As community managers are able to develop a strong iterative strategy, cultivate advocates into leaders, cement policy and guidelines, encourage interaction that develops strong content from numerous areas within the community, and draw members into the 1% and 9% groups, they will realize that they are changing from administrators back into advisors. This is evident when a community manager transitions from recruiting and aggregating content to engaging, facilitating, and creating content as a way to influence the contributions of all of the membership (customers and internal teams).

Content and Programming

When we start a community for our company, we generally find that we contribute an average of 70% of the content in the message boards and other content areas. It takes a long time—and much effort on both the company's and members' sides—to get to the level of 50/50 or content parity. Depending on the community, it has taken from months to sometimes years to find the magic balance of content to reach the tipping point. When you do eventually reach parity, though, it gains momentum and we have found that you are able to swing over to the customers/members providing more of the content than you are. This is good thing, as the general perception seems to be that their content contributions are more valuable than yours and carry more weight and less spin. This isn't bad news, so embrace it as best you can.

This is the point where it becomes necessary to find ways to surface the best content—that of value to the objectives of the community members and those of the company as well, so that it is easy to find for all members amidst a river of information flow. This may be done organically by the community advocates and/or power users or may need to be done through other mechanisms, such as community managers manually pointing it out on a regular basis or creating system capabilities that surface the content on the website or through e-mail newsletters that select content based on certain criteria such as views, replies, comments, positive ratings, and so on.

Enjoy the activity and engagement around the content and find ways to mine the data for information that can be turned into products for your internal teams. Then work to leverage the engagement to co-develop a large portion of your content and close the communication loop whereby the content product that is not returned outright to the community is evidence that you are listening to its members and where they want to go with the product and your company.

Policies and Governance

The term we use as guidance for when we create policies and governance is "minimal sufficiency"—not in the context of mathematical equations and statistics, but more from the perspective of creating governance that has just enough control to maintain order (with the obvious intent to protect intellectual property and confidential information for the sake of the company, our legal department, and the membership). This allows the culture to thrive and the community leaders and members to engage and innovate with regard to our products and the community initiative overall. We have been pleasantly surprised time and time again by the ingenuity and innovative spirit of our community members in how they leverage the communities and the engagement within. Over time though, as a community grows and matures, you will most likely find that you have to revisit, adjust, tweak, and yes, increase the level of governance—and the policies to support these new governance requirements will increase as well. Inevitably, as your membership grows there will be people who try to push the envelope and test your governance and the leadership to guide it for other than altruistic intent and the overall benefit of the community. In our communities, we do an annual review of the guidelines that support our terms and conditions, and are in the process of establishing an ombudsmen council so grievances and issues can be raised fairly and within the purview of the community.

Tools

To initially grow and develop your community, you may use simple tools, whether they are hosted on the premises, in a software as a service (SaaS) platform, or by leveraging one of the free tools made available by any number of online collaboration companies. The reason to strive for simplicity is to make it as easy as possible for the community members to find content, engage with each other, and eventually contribute content—which should be the goal of every engagement initiative in an online community. The tools, meant to extend whatever would be normal face-to-face interaction into the online space, will mature as the need arises or there are opportunities to leapfrog to a more complex tool that is also easy to use and administer. Initially you may have just a home base for your members but then branch out to leverage other social channels to engage members (and potential members) on a platform of their choice and draw them back to the home base in a hub and spoke model, which is fairly common today. Eventually, as the content and engagement develop and progress (including video service, enabling ideation for the community, serving freeware and shareware, developing solutions collaboratively, and engaging in customer validation of soon to be delivered releases), then the complexity of the tools used within the community will have to mature in sync in order to provide these services in an easy and intuitive way so that the engagement initiative works and develops value for the participants.

Metrics and Measurement

In a developing community, you will probably focus on basic numbers to assess your communities—membership and participation most likely. Perhaps you will include some measurement around perceived value—very likely anecdotal stories from community leaders and members as they occur within the interaction (quotes and success stories). Increasing membership and activity are good, solid indicators that you are doing the correct things to help your community succeed. Metrics and measurements are discussed in greater detail later on in the book, but for the sake of examining maturity you will eventually find that measuring the community against itself will no longer suffice. The community can't be viewed as existing only for the sake of serving the community—part of the strategy and the plan should be that as you ingrain the community and the engagement into the various ways of conducting business with your company, the measurements need to mature and become more complex. They must measure the business impact against the goals and objectives of the community. While community is often seen as nice and sometimes necessary, the point of supporting a community and engaging the members is ultimately to drive the business—for the mutual benefit of both the company and the customer no doubt, but it's for the business overall.

Assessing Your Community Maturity

It's important to review your current state and assess your community to understand where you are and where to focus your efforts and resources, since there often seems to never be enough time or as many resources desired to get all of the necessary work done to ensure that your community is successful. Here we will explore how to start assessing your community with regard to maturity and foundational characteristics and examine several methods and tools that can be used for that purpose.

We like to do *traffic-light visualization reports* (Figure 4-3), in which we assign green, yellow, or red ratings to different aspects within the communities, such as leadership, engagement, and the various content initiatives we have that span the certain communities. It is a simple way to display visually the relative health of each aspect of the community. Although subjective in nature, the ratings are assigned by the community managers who work in and live and breathe the communities each and every day, so that their ratings carry significant weight and can be verbally substantiated through qualitative anecdote if quantitative data are not available for that aspect. It is a good, simple way to display the health ratings in aggregate, whether for a community, all communities related to a business unit, or across the entire company. Your company may not see each area of your overall community as separate or individual communities, but given our customer-led, vendor-supported model, we do. So being able to roll the information together in a way that is simple and makes sense is important to us given the complexity associated with the model we have in place today.

Communities	Business Unit	
	Community X	Community Y
Community Activities		
Membership Count	2113	2383
Customer Board	Green	Red
Webcasts	Green	Yellow
Message Boards	Green	Green
Blogs	Green	N/A
Code Sharing / Scripts	Green	N/A
Regional Groups	Green	Red

Figure 4-3. Sample traffic-light visualization report for relative health across rating areas within the communities

Every eighteen months, we host a collaborative event for our community leaders known as the Community Leadership Summit (CLS). The event is held in conjunction with our company's premier event, CA World, which brings our customers together with the company, partners, analysts and other thought leaders to connect, learn, and share knowledge and industry best practices around our products and solutions. A featured speaker at CLS was Nancy White of Full Circle Associates, who provided an information nugget that I will now include as a part of our reporting and analytics process to assess our communities, in conjunction with the competencies outlined by The Community Roundtable.

What Nancy showed to our community leaders was a *spidergram* (aka *radar chart*) as a way to visualize subjective maturity ratings for each of the competencies. I say *subjective* because we do not yet have a way to normalize or standardize the ratings quantitatively across the broad spectrum of communities we sponsor and collaborate with. As such, what I've done is assign a rating of the maturity competencies with a simple rating on a scale of 1 through 10. This allows for a decent level of granularity while keeping the example for the book easy to understand. Take a look at Figure 4-4 for how the data need to be placed in a spreadsheet to be converted into a radar chart.

Table 4-1. Chart of assessment categories from The Community Roundtable Community Maturity Model (CMM) and sample subjective ratings on a scale of 1 to 10 for an onboard or formative community. This table corresponds to the Figure 4-4 spidergram

CMM Assessment Category	Subjective Rating
Strategy	8
Leadership	6
Culture	8
Community Management	9
Content & Programming	5
Policies & Governance	5
Tools	5
Metrics & Measurement	4

Using these numbers to create the visualization is easy in your favorite spreadsheet application, and it is also very easily done on a whiteboard or with paper and pen. While it does not roll up or scale the way our traffic-light reports do, it does provide a great view of where progress has been made, success achieved, and where there is room for improvement within the community. If you are able to build data out and conduct periodic assessments, you can also use different colors for the lines to represent two time periods (e.g., year over year) to show the progress, or lack of progress, with regard to the competencies/areas examined (for example, comparing Figures 4-4 and 4-5).

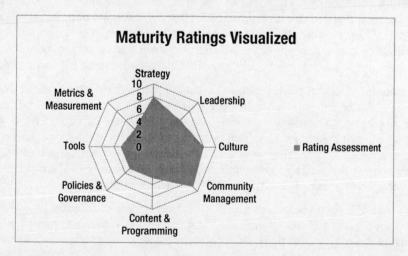

Figure 4-4. Sample spidergram for an onboard or formative community corresponding to the ratings in Table 4-1

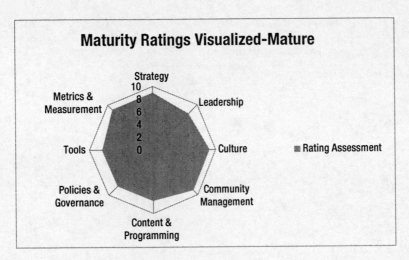

Figure 4-5. Sample spidergram for a mature community

Figure 4-4 represents a community that is newly formed, with strengths in areas such as strategy, culture, and community management and with some progress in developing the leadership. The spidergram shows where the work is needed as well: content and programming, policies and governance, and tools. Metrics and measurement fall behind as there is not yet much to measure. As the focus areas progress, there will be an increased need to measure the community and progress to analytics based-decision guidance, and you will also see the central shaded area expand across the chart as the areas improve.

A mature community is shown in Figure 4-5. This community has had the time and attention needed to reach this stage and grow out in all of the desired competencies. There is still work that can be done to advance in certain areas, but in this instance it can be seen that the leadership, community managers, and members have made a concerted effort toward a balanced and active community.

This representational device can be carried out to whatever degree is necessary or desired by your organization. If you decide to adopt this model for assessing your community maturity, you may wish to carry it to the next level by adjusting your rating assessment thresholds for each stage across the life cycle, creating different views and thresholds for forming, established, and mature communities as you move the goalposts and reset expectations during the iterative process of managing communities through the life cycle.

A team at CA Technologies devised a method and tool to assess the vitality of technical communities of practice. The method is extremely granular in its assessment, sorting the many different aspects of the community interaction into six major groups defined by distinctive characteristics: foundational, communications, activity, dialogue and decision making, governance and metrics, and knowledge management (Table 4-2).[4]

Table 4-2. Six Major Groups of Community Interactions with Defining Characteristics in the CA Technologies Scheme

Foundational	Communications	Activity
Attendance	Recognition	Individual Activity
Participation	Organization of Communications	Balance in Member Activity
Funding		Outside Activities
Charter	Executive Exposure	Crossover Activities
Group Membership	Celebrate Accomplishments	Mentoring
Executive Sponsorship		Coaching
Dedicated Community Leader		Community Activity
Recruitment		Community Role Sharing
Social Fabric		Consensus Building
Unique Business Need		Professional Standing
Goals		Challenge/Solution
ROI		

Dialogue and Decision Making	Governance and Metrics	Knowledge Management
Clear Defined Decision Making	Governance	Push/Pull Technology
Subgroup Leaders	Metric Availability	Accessibility
Decision-Making Structure	Community Outputs Are Relevant and Respect Participant Efforts	Usability
Dialogue Focus		Technical Infrastructure
Dialogue Structure	Number of Active Discussions	Technical Vitality and Thought Leadership
Constructive Discussion		Knowledge Management
Technical Reach and Influence	Average Response Rates	Patents
		Innovation
		Tacit Knowledge

[4]United States Patent Application, Strong et al., US 2013/0089850 A1, Published April 11, 2013.

The CA Technologies method weights rating assessments across the group-ings in Table 4-2 to calculate an overall score. Although the first iteration of this tool is still subjective in nature, the weighting makes it a powerful method of evaluation for technical communities. The patent states that this "tool may be configured to determine where a particular technical community is in the lifecycle, assess the technical community, and/or provide remediation by highlighting opportune areas of improvement, thereby facilitating continuous improvement and value to business."[5] Tools and methods such as this can help community managers create and develop strategy and tactics for progression, as well as demonstrate both the current and potential value of community content and engagement.

Summary

There are many different aspects to life cycle and maturity within online communities.

- As with the communities we live in, online communities progress through a life cycle—one that may renew when certain efforts or concepts are applied.

- They don't mature evenly in most cases—they mature across several competencies at varying rates depen-dent on the people, the culture, the tools, and other resources.

- Measuring maturity is an important part of understanding where the community is in its life cycle and where to apply your focus and resources to ensure the community thrives.

---

[5]Ibid. 8.

Community Management

A Differentiator in Successful B2B Communities

Art and science have their meeting point in method.

—Edward Bulwer-Lytton, *Caxtoniana*

Community management is a nascent discipline—part science, part art. The one constant appears to be the entrepreneurial nature of the practice as it has evolved over the years. In any given day, a variety of challenges present themselves both from internal and external entities that need to be addressed or possibly even developed into "crisis-tunities"[1]—where what appears as an outright crisis is managed through a coordinated team effort to become an opportunity. An investment in people who engage your customers is an investment in your brand around the concepts of influence and, more importantly, trust—factors that can significantly affect both your top and bottom lines, through new contracts and revenue protection/retention alike.

---

[1]Urban Dictionary. Accessed June 24, 2013. www.urbandictionary.com/define.php?term=Crisitunity

An Investment in Social Capital

Having people available to your community members—whom they get to know and understand how to interact with—humanizes your company and helps turn the investment in your communities into social capital.[2]

Brian Solis, principal analyst at Altimeter Group and author of *What's the Future of Business*, wonderfully explains this benefit in terms of *three pillars of influence* (Figure 5-1).[3] The three pillars are *reach, resonance*, and *relevance*—and investing in each as a form of capital through the proper actions creates the desired effect of increasing influence."Digital capitalization is laying a foundation for expanding the need to cultivate and participate, not only in the real world, but also in the online networks and communities that can benefit us personally and professionally."[4] The increase of influence online increases trust, which is the base for improved brand perception and reputation and strengthens relationships (Figure 5-1).

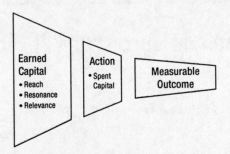

Figure 5-1. The pillars of influence—reach, resonance, and relevance—translate to a funnel of measurable outcome for the benefit of the business

The need for human interaction and the desire to do good within a community can be monetized for a company within an online community. Soft skills are respected but not always considered part of the money-making ability of a business. They should be, for they are the way you can take earned capital through online efforts and combine them with capital investment efforts for measureable outcomes for the benefit of the business.

---

[2]Tristan Claridge. "Social Capital Is About the Value of Social Networks, Bonding Similar People and Bridging between Diverse People, with Norms of Reciprocity." Available at: www.socialcapitalresearch.com/definition.html.

[3]Brian Solis."The Rise of Digital Influence." The Altimeter Group, March 21,2012. Available at: www.slideshare.net/Altimeter/the-rise-of-digital-influence.

[4]Brian Solis. "Social Capital: The Currency of the Social Economy." The Altimeter Group, March 3, 2010. Available at: www.briansolis.com/2010/03/social-capital-the-currency-of-digital,citizens/.

Trust is one of the more critical factors here. It is critical to keep pace with the speed of technology development and the speed of social interaction—both of which can be near real time. Stephen M. R. Covey explains the economic factors related to trust in greater detail—and he turns what has been considered a nice, warm, and fuzzy concept into something that can be "tangible and quantifiable." The basis of this construct is that trust affects two business factors—speed and cost.[5]

The higher level of trust, the faster you can do business, which keeps the cost of doing business low. Online communities and active community management are an investment in digital capital to build trust and drive your brand and your business forward. One of the linchpins to achieving success in building trust is your online community manager(s).

▓ **Remember**   A good community manager is key to building trust with your stakeholders. Choose that person well.

Community Management—Active and Passive

Action may not always bring happiness; but there is no happiness without action.

—Benjamin Disraeli, *Lothair*

There are two general approaches to community management—passive and active. Passive community management is when you establish a community environment and then see whether or not it develops organically. Perhaps you add content now and then but you rely on the community membership to find its own way to success. It's akin to inviting people to a party but letting them find out what it's for on their own and not providing a host to introduce the guests and get the party started. You can hope for success but there are not necessarily plans or strategy associated with the chosen path—especially because the path and the desired outcome are not being communicated to the audience.

---

[5]Stephen M. R. Covey. *The Speed of Trust.* New York: Free Press, 2008, p. 13.

Though passive community management may work in certain circumstances in networks where completely organic growth is possible ("life will find a way"), it is very likely a rare creature with B2B companies. You can find numerous attempts nonetheless—community sites spread across the Internet and corporate intranets with members, yet with very little content and even less interaction. Imagine trying to sell a product without investing in a sales force.

A once-successful community had benefited from active community management but lost that benefit when the community manager was removed from his role because of a loss of sponsorship. Tom Humbarger watched the community he had created, analyzed, and nurtured decline over time with slower membership growth, declining number of visits, a drop in the number of page views per visit, and less time spent on the site per visit (Figure 5-2).[6] He writes: "It's interesting to discover that a neglected community will indeed continue to function without a dedicated community manager. However, the results are lackluster and the picture is not 'pretty'."

Conversely, when dedicated community managers apply the proper principles (i.e., active community management), their actions can drive membership growth, increase activity, improve interaction, and demonstrate the value of the collaboration. Active community management can either augment or even make up for inherent shortfalls in whatever process or systems are in place to support the interaction among community members.

Let's get started on the finer focus. We are going to drill in on:

- Traits of successful B2B community managers

- Where to find a community manager

- Racing teams and community management (That's right! NASCAR!)

- Established principles of community management—the tip of the iceberg

- Why communities fail

---

[6]Tom Humbarger. "The Importance of Active Community Management." Posted January 13, 2009. Available at: http://tomhumbarger.wordpress.com/2009/01/13/the-importance-of-active-community-management-proved-with-real-data/

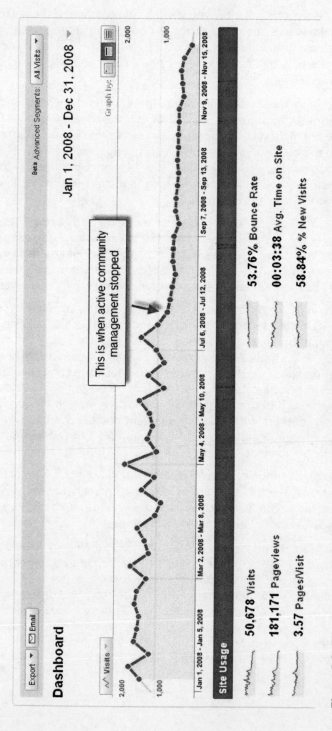

Figure 5-2. The decline of a community without active community management. (Reprinted by permission of Tom Humbarger.)

With the information in this chapter, you will be able to understand better the goal and potential positive outcomes of active community management. What is that goal? The goal is to build initial activity to a manageable level and then move the community activities to a new stage in the lifecycle and through various levels of maturity.

This objective to increase the benefits to customers and the corporation for an improved customer experience and better business is part of that larger, long-term goal. Empathy and the desire to help are two of the key factors here, for example, and the quid pro quo nature of these engagements is essential to building trust and social capital, which can then be converted into monetary equity and shareholder value. This concept is a constant in this book and in the practice of community management.

Keep in mind that active community management never ends or reaches completion—it is cyclical in nature. When you reach a new level of accomplishment, the person managing and steering the community needs to revert to the basic principles of building up the interaction via collaborative initiatives from a new start to the next level of maturity in the community lifecycle.

Much of what we will be examining may vary based on the community model, governance model, systems, community maturity, and other factors particular to your company and your business. As a result, you may weigh the various factors differently when evaluating community managers and structuring your team. However, you will notice certain constants that transcend the differentiating factors enumerated in Chapter 2—such as goals, audience, model, and maturity. Although much of this may seem like another version of Community 101, it's often the repetition with a slightly different perspective that brings the aha! moments in recognizing the value of communities—in B2B or any other business environment for that matter.

One of our veteran community managers at CA Technologies, Chris Hackett, exemplifies the traits desired in an online community manager. Here he tells how he engaged the community actively to help build membership, activity, and value, and how he rallied internal teams to engage members/customers:

> *When I first started working as a CA Technologies community manager, our mission was to invigorate the tempo and style of community interaction to meet the needs and expectations of today's customers. It was time to ramp up from the world of quarterly webcasts to the world of message boards, blogs and wikis. Now we focus our efforts on keeping our customers engaged in real time, and whenever members need additional insight on a problem we're ready to throw the right CA expert into the mix. Thanks to this commitment, our communities are thriving.*

—Chris Hackett
Principal, Community Management
CA Technologies

Desirable Traits Found in Successful B2B Community Managers

In an ideal scenario, the community manager will have an extended team to rely on. But the community manager is the central personality that will drive the interaction with community members—customers, partners, and prospects. It takes a particular type of person, with certain qualities, to be able to act as the linchpin of the team and ensure an active and successful community (Figure 5-3).

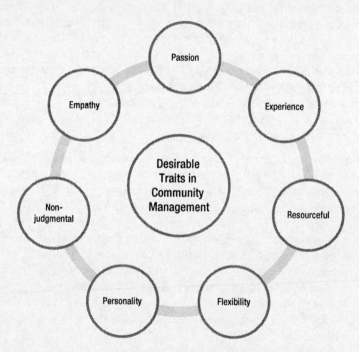

Figure 5-3. The desirable traits found in successful online community managers

Many people have examined and noted the qualities and traits of a successful or highly effective community manager. We have our own list, which follows. It appears that many people have trouble visualizing a potential community manager, yet all of us know when we've met one in our past experience. Here are the characteristics to look for:

Passion/Affinity. With any community that develops in the physical or offline world, it is the common bond that brings people to the location and the interaction that keeps them there (and coming back). This is no different with online communities in the digital world. One of the aspects that can help keep the community tied together and on track is if it's clear the community manager cares either professionally or personally about the primary topic the community is founded on and operates around. That interest and passion translates into action and engenders trust with the membership—and it is not something that is easily "faked" for very long. As the novelist E. M. Forster reputedly once said, "One person with passion is better than forty people merely interested."

Depth of Experience. It's often suggested to us that Millennials (those born after 1982 or thereabouts) be brought in to manage communities owing to their immersion and familiarity with social channels and online interaction. This is a bit of a contentious subject that calls a person's experience and capabilities into question. You have to look at this in the context of your particular business and desired outcomes from your community investment. Apart from concerns about callowness and the potential difference between B2C and B2B communities, interns and Millennials can bring a lot of energy and innovative ideas to the table when managing communities and working across social channels. However, you'll often find that having someone with a varied experience across lines of business (marketing, support, operations, etc.) augments these other traits and establishes a level of trust and confidence with both community members and sponsors.

Our community management team at CA Technologies has, with its current community management team, on average 2 to 4 years of community management experience and 10 to 15 years of professional experience in marketing, support, sales, product management, and information systems. You may also wish to take into consideration the level of experience of the average community member—very often they may seek out or share more with peers from a shared background more easily because there is already established common ground. Within our own communities, for example, are the communities formed for the mainframe products. From what we've seen, people who have worked with mainframe solutions have a distinct community sense and language based on their knowledge of and experience with mainframe technology in general.

Entrepreneurial Spirit/Resourcefulness. When starting a new community or even a new initiative for an established community, it will often seem as if you are starting a new business. A community manager has to create the plan, get buy in and sponsorship, market the plan, execute the plan, and then report the results—all of which can be notoriously challenging in today's corporate world of limited resources. Being able to deliver successfully on this routine in a large organization, despite its silos and bureaucracy, can be incredibly challenging. The ability to come up with new and creative ways to leverage existing tools and channels is invaluable. And the ability to maintain the spirit of entrepreneurship is critical given the cyclical nature of communities and new content and interaction projects that arise as teams within the business seek to engage the community. The limitations of the systems and business processes will often ensure that community managers and business leads will have to think "outside of the box" in order to achieve the goals as set forth by the business and community members alike.

Flexibility/Ability to Balance Art and Science. Much of this book is about the *soft arts* that accompany and drive success in community management. Examples of soft arts are relationship building, networking, objections handling, brokering engagement, the ability to display empathy, and so on. The next level of proficiency is being able to advertise that success back out to the sponsors and membership, which relates more to the science of numbers and analytics. Analytics-based decision making will help you drive the direction of current and future initiatives and guide the community to success overall. A community manager, therefore, needs to be able to develop, understand, interpret and translate the numbers into easily understood terms.

In terms of proving progress back to the business, you'll have lots of anecdotal evidence if the community is successful. But being able to establish solid key performance indicators (KPIs), map these to the investment, and establish return on investment (ROI) figures are paramount—they allow a community manager to construct a narrative around the community data that relates the interaction to the business in a way that makes sense to the business. Your community manager will need an understanding of the business—both strategy and operations—to come up with good KPIs and ROI figures that apply to the business. Some measurements matter more than others from a business perspective, and building these out can allow greater and quicker understanding of the value of community to the business. This can be one of the more elusive achievements, even when the will and understanding to succeed are present. This is primarily because there can be challenges in understanding evolving strategies and also in obtaining access to the right data within the organization.

Personality/Ability to Connect. Another critical trait is to be able to make and maintain connections within a community. These connections can be numerous and complex. They include connections between members and the business, between members and other members, between members and the content, between your community and external communities in social channels, and so on. Although a community manager does not have to be an extremely outgoing person in his or her personal life, the ability to be or transform into a digital extrovert is imperative to facilitating and enhancing the activities and interactions in an online community. This can be particularly handy when dealing with people who are hard to reach or when a negative or disruptive situation may occur (see the next trait). Personal connections allow you to accentuate the positive and downplay the negative. The difference between just having a website or a social channel and having a community that engages and delivers value to the business and the members is the connections that are made between the members and the business.

Nonjudgmental/Ability to Manage Personalities. A good community manager will be able to elevate the positive comments but also mitigate any negative, emotional, or controversial and provoking statements that can cause strife among the membership, decrease interaction, and limit the value proposition of participating in the community.

An online community will have many varied personalities. These personalities will range from your proponents and advocates on one side to detractors and trolls on the other. One of the most important aspects of this trait in practice is to avoid getting drawn down to the level of the detractors as they try to disrupt positive collaborative efforts. Discourse of a controversial nature is important and needed for innovative efforts within the community—and it is the job of the community manager to drive and solicit such discourse—but it is important to be able to filter the positive from the negative, and the professional from the personal.

Not many brands (if any) can have all proponents and no detractors. The current economy and a company's past can bring a great deal of history into a relationship with its customer base, so some people will find it extremely difficult to embrace the brand, no matter how far it may have evolved since the original or perceived transgression occurred. It can be tough to "hug someone who doesn't want to be hugged," so establishing as many positive connections across the membership allows such people to still reach out to each other and interact in a positive and collaborative nature.

Note "If Passion drives, let Reason hold the Reins." —Benjamin Franklin, *Autobiography*

Empathy/Desire to Help. The element that ties the rest of these together is the inherent desire to help your members, sponsors, and colleagues in many ways—sometimes in ways that will often surprise you with their unusual or repeated requests for information or assistance. Having a genuine interest in assisting them in understanding community concepts and values, as well as in navigating the environment and avoiding pitfalls, is *priceless*. Along with personality, experience, and passion, empathy truly engenders trust with internal and external sponsors and, most importantly, the membership a community manager guides and serves. Members will recognize the "pay-it-forward" attitude and will reciprocate it in their day-to-day interactions with each other. This helps greatly with moving members from the 90 percent of lurkers to be part of the 9 percent of occasional contributors. This is the 1/9/90 rule of online communities, something you should be aware of.[7] This rule states that

---

[7] "1% Rule." Available at: http://en.wikipedia.org/wiki/1%25_rule_(Internet_culture)

1% of people create content, 9 percent edit or modify that content, and 90 percent view the content without contributing. Through empathy, the number of people in each percentage range can be shifted from lurkers on to various levels of contribution.

So how do we sum up this section? As Daniel Pink points out in his book *A Whole New Mind*,[8] the age of "left-brain thinking" and working to develop single-silo technical skills to be leveraged throughout an entire career is waning. "Right-brain thinkers"—more creative and intuitive—are expected to be more likely to attain professional success and personal satisfaction. This dovetails nicely with community management, as many of the traits that are embodied in successful community managers are aligned with those Pink outlines as the six fundamentally human abilities that are essential for professional success and personal fulfillment.

You're not looking for an accountant here—you're looking for a free thinker who espouses as many of the traits just described as possible. You're looking for a person who can switch hats, without blinking an eye, and engender each of these essential elements as often as needed.

Where Do I Look?

So now that you know what to look for in your ideal candidate, where do you start looking? Is it better to look internally or externally? Let's tally the pros and cons of each.

Experience has found that internal candidates have had much success in adapting to the role—primarily owing to their knowledge, experience, and existing relationships across the business. This allows for a quicker ramp-up time in a large, complex organization, something that can be daunting to navigate without prior similar experience. This is definitely a route to consider when seeking community managers and others to support the overall effort—and is something that might be more prevalent within larger companies. Unless they are able to have an employee wear yet another hat within the company, small enterprises may have to look externally for a candidate unless there is an "up and comer" from a junior role ready for the responsibility. The wearing of multiple hats can lead to burnout and often leave one of the areas under the hats with less attention than another—something not very productive for online communities.

Much of this takes on more import within B2B communities, as the products tend to be more "niche" focused and less well known than many commercial products found that are supported in B2C type communities or social channels. This generally leads to smaller audiences than in many B2C communities,

---

[8]Daniel Pink. *A Whole New Mind*. New York: Riverhead Books, 2006, p. 3.

and the audience tends to be professional in nature—related to a specific product of offering. Knowledge of the products can become very important because they can be very unique—the product itself is the matter of importance for the community as opposed to a consumer product such as blue jeans— jeans may be jeans, but then the brand may play a significant role in experience. So hiring from within may be desirable if this is the case.

If you open your search to external candidates, the same principles apply. One thing to take into account is that, while communities and social media are very much related, they are somewhat different disciplines. Although many of the social channels strive for engagement and interaction (but are not yet quite there), communities depend on this level of interaction for their very survival. In looking back on our traits for success in B2B communities, "depth of experience" is something that definitely matters, and having the ability to connect on many levels is paramount to establish and maintain the relationships necessary for success in community efforts.

B2B relationships between vendors and customers are different from many B2C relationships because the contractual terms of the relationship is years in duration rather than hours/days/weeks/months (although this is changing in our industry with the rise of SaaS, MaaS, and other cloud-enabled technology that may have shorter contracts, which can make it easier to switch from one vendor to another). It is a different scope of time and duration than many other types of interaction across social channels. Though B2C relationships may be based on products similar to B2B products, the contracts are generally structured differently and may not be as "sticky." The relationships may not last long compared with B2B business engagements. The takeaway here is that you may want to find someone familiar with the landscape within your industry and how other communities are formed and managed—or find someone who can learn quickly or adapt relevant knowledge and experience to a competitive advantage.

If you are looking externally, you should look to swim where the practitioners swim and observe how they interact among their peers. There are many communities of community practitioners out there on Google+, LinkedIn, and some outside of the traditional social channels, such as The Community Roundtable. These groups may provide candidates (such as when you are in LinkedIn and can see their profile/resume in addition to their interactions and posts) or perhaps even offer suggestions of who might be right to fill the role. As it is still a relatively recent job role, many people who are community managers know and network with other community managers as a matter of practice—and many folks in these communities are open to new opportunities and experiences.

No matter where you look, you should definitely consider the desirable traits as discussed earlier in this chapter and seek out "right-brain" entrepreneurs to lead your community management efforts. This is your first investment in social capital in terms of building trust and deep relationships with your customer base. It should be noted that hiring a community manager is not just a "seat to fill"—as you'll see, this person becomes the focal point for a team effort in your investment into digital capital and trust. We have sometimes accepted individuals from other teams during restructuring efforts within the company; though it has worked out well in some cases, it has not worked out as well in others. You will have to make a judgment call here—and it's not always an easy one—though usually it is best to "trust your gut" with regard to what you are trying to accomplish with your business and your community.

One way to identify if your candidate meets the needs is, of course, the interview process. Beyond the standard questions you might have, you might be able to ask some questions that go a level up in focus around community management, such as:

- What made you choose this path as a career?
- What communities have you managed and what were your responsibilities?
- What did you set out to achieve with the community and did you actually achieve it?
- How do you see those lessons applying to our company and community?
- How do you see online community supporting our business strategy?
- What metrics will you use to align the community with business strategy?
- How will you communicate metrics/updates/opportunities to the c-suite?
- Are you familiar with the legal/compliance considerations for our industry and how that may apply to an online community?
- What are your views on the technology that supports the community interaction?

These questions are just a sampling of what may apply to your instance or opportunity—from our own list of questions we use to interview candidates. From this, you should be able to see how inside knowledge, experience, and expertise either in the subject matter that is the base for the community or in community management would allow you a quicker return on your investment in a particular human resource.

So as we stated in the beginning of this section—one answer to where to look is, "it depends." Of course, the answer we would suggest is you look "everywhere," possibly to the ends of the earth, and be open to new concepts in order to find the person who matches the traits most likely to fit your community audience and its stated goals. It can make a significant difference for your community, your business goals, and both the top and bottoms lines for your company.

Racing—A Team Effort Much Like Community Management

Community management is often seen as a solo effort—a single person's time and responsibility. Though the community manager will certainly be a central, visible person and handle a large part of the responsibility for the maintenance and overall health of the community, it is hardly an individual effort. Plain and simple, it takes a team to host a viable, transparent community in the B2B space.

Whether you consider NASCAR or Formula One (I'll let you choose based on your preference), they can be seen as individual events—a driver and his or her car engaged in competition against other cars and drivers. Despite the driver being a central and extremely important figure, he or she requires a large team in support. Team players include the owner, sponsor, team manager, crew chief, car chief, driver, pit crew, engineers, mechanics, and a host of other folks to get the car and driver to the race and around the track. It's all community management in a macro sense. Let's look at the roles, sticking with the car-racing analogy.

Owner. The *owner* is the "boss" of the community. This is the person who provides overall guidance for how the community grows and where it goes. Who fulfills this role may vary depending on your model and governance structure chosen for your community. Though some companies may establish this role internally, some models include shared ownership or even enabling the community to act as the owners themselves. Some are customer-based and many are company-based. At CA Technologies, we have chosen a blended model to maximize external advocacy efforts and keep everyone feeling like they've got a piece of the pie. So in our communities, we have an internal executive owner (such as the CEO or an executive vice president over all of the communities) and then community board officers (customers and partners—external entities) who share in the ownership of the communities.

Sponsor. Though some communities may rely on outside *sponsorship* for funding and marketing support (such as in dues), here we are talking about internal executive-level sponsors. Internal executive sponsorship (from our own experience) is critical in terms of financial backing and also in communicating the value of participating in community activity to senior leadership. Top-down communications helps bring new teams and content into the community, which helps bring in new membership and new activity. That keeps moving the community along the path of the community lifecycle.

Driver/Car. This is the community itself—the rest of the team is responsible for making sure it's designed well, operates at peak efficiency, doesn't wind up in any accidents or crashes, and is part of a winning program.

Team Manager. This is the community manager. It is the role that has to keep the owner and sponsor aware of key trends and opportunities as well as ensure the rest of the team is connected and contributing to the community and being responsive. Picture this person as the DMZ between your community and the business it is supporting.

Crew Chief/Mechanics. These are product experts who participate and contribute on a daily basis by either responding to member inquiries or introducing new content around areas such as product direction and so forth. They are the people who produce the content that creates the basis for interaction within the community. "People come for the content and stay for the community."[9]

Pit Crew. These are participants from the support organization—subject matter experts who primarily respond to member inquiries. Responsiveness is a critical factor here, and success in this form of interaction provides the base for all other levels of interaction.

Car Chief/Engineers. These folks keep the community environment tuned and performing as expected. Though the community is never based on the technology or the platform, it is the platform that allows the membership to engage and interact—therefore it's a somewhat paradoxical situation. In addition to supporting the community platform and making sure the interaction is able to take place, they also provide access to and possibly even help crunch the numbers to provide metrics and develop data in support of ROI analysis.

Fans. They are pretty much the whole *raison d'être*—one of the primary reasons why the race takes place to begin with. They are the reason for the community, the community manager, and if you want to go to the highest level, the company. These are your customers and your community members. They, through their company, provide the revenue to make everything possible, including online community interaction. You don't just want customers, or even just satisfied customers—you want "raving fans"[10] who will act as brand advocates and carry your message out for you.

---

[9] Vanessa DiMauro. "Building Online Communities for Business" (Online Blog). Posted June 17, 2011. Available at: http://blog.leadernetworks.com/2011/06/people-come-for-content-and-stay-for.html.

[10] Ken Blanchard. *Raving Fans*. New York: William Morrow and Company, 1993.

Don't Forget Content

As stated before, members come and join for the content, but they stay for the community. To have them come in the first place, you need to deliver value to the community with topnotch content—information that answers questions, solves problems, sparks innovation, and in general keeps people coming back. As with a racing team, there are some key front people who will be delivering content, but there are many more working behind the scenes in a coordinated manner to ensure value is delivered to as many members as possible through the various content channels (message boards, blogs, wikis, newsletters, webcasts, etc.).

It is the job of anyone and everyone in a company to contribute content. It's up to the community manager to guide them to the right place to engage community members and succeed in adding value. There is opportunity for everyone to provide something of value in online community—and to do so in a way that matches their personality. You don't want to bring a potential or actual content contributor outside of his or her comfort zone all the time. Though it can be a growth experience to do so occasionally, you want to make sure that the content channel within the community is suited not only for the type of content but also the author/creator of that content. Someone who tends to be a bit on the introverted side may be well and fine with answering message board inquiries, but it could be an entirely stress-inducing experience to have him or her present on a webcast with potentially hundreds of your community members in attendance. You want to create quality content, not make your employees live in fear to the point where they won't contribute ever again. The community manager, working in coordination with the business they support and the members, should have a content plan—that is, a document or content map where there is detail around what content will be shared in each channel, by whom, how often and, most importantly, for what reason. There should be a justification for each effort made within the community—even it if is an experiment or proof of concept effort.

Understand that there will be different levels or amounts of content contributed by each tier (Figure 5-4). Much of this depends on your community and the focus that is required of the content, but as a general rule, you should look to the higher levels within your organization for thought leadership and strategy material and then get more granular from there as you move down throughout the roles and job functions in the pyramid. Seek management for the translation between strategy and tactical level detail—and the general employee base (in our case, development, support, etc.) for the true tactical level detail around the discussion topic. The type of content relates to the amount in that there will most likely be the need for much more technical content than that of a thought leadership nature.

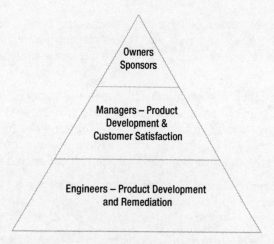

Figure 5-4. Pyramid of content contribution. As you move down the chain in an organization, you will often find that the amount of content contributed will increase per level—and it will differ in nature as well

Something important for the community manager to recognize and embrace as he or she is developing the content plan and launching an initiative is to ensure that the effort is sustainable. Too often content initiatives are thought to be "fire and forget" efforts and they are most certainly not. They need to be monitored and nurtured to ensure they continue to deliver value to the company and community members alike. If the content is the reason a member joins the community, and then the content is either sporadically posted or dries up altogether, you may lose a member if there is no other intrinsic value in his or her participation.

The Established Principles of Community Management

You try, you fail, you pick yourself up, and you try again. Persistence is unbelievably powerful.

—Howard A. Tullman, President and CEO
Tribeca Flashpoint
Media Arts Academy

There are many different factors involved in what comprises a community or what makes it succeed. That makes it difficult to define explicitly the proper principles and methods that guarantee community success. Though online community building is a nascent practice, and has yet to be fully developed, there are many best practices and lessons that can help a community manager succeed. These will also help executives understand the many challenges that may be faced along the road to a successful community and the lifecycle it will follow.

As found in the State of Community Management reports, the folks at The Community Roundtable paint community leaders as explorers, builders, and translators.[11] Anyone looking to take on or understand the role of community management in today's business landscape should ponder that statement well while examining the breadth and depth of the principles that follow.

The basic principle community managers should follow is to "be yourself." This won't be hard if you or your community manager has the desired traits previously discussed. They are the basis for the principles listed here.

What follows is by no means an exhaustive list—it could be and should be added to on a regular basis as you find and establish new principles. The field is so young that, if you are diligent, you will come up with new ideas/principles/practices no one has yet employed.

Community managers will need to be able to:

- Understand their audience and where to find potential members and grow the community—and then proactively leverage that to build it up through the lifecycle.

- Understand the business being supported and what the key measurements are that need to be attained in support of strategic and tactical goals.

- Know how activities and programs scale to build them organically and effectively so they become more easily sustained—most community program efforts are not "fire and forget"—and they succeed more often if they are ingrained into the daily workflow of an employee and also as a member so they are not seen as additional work.

- Know how to drive participation effectively in the community from both internal and external members, act as advisor to both audiences, and engage in proactive conflict resolution when needed.

---

[11]Rachel Happe and Jim Storer. "State of Community Management 2012." The Community Roundtable. Posted March 26, 2012. Available at: www.slideshare.net/rhappe/2012-state-of-community-management-12162160, p. 20.

- Display persistence when faced with adversity and/or setbacks—challenges will present themselves constantly, and they will vary in size and scope and come from both internal and external entities.

- Demonstrate the ROI both in qualitative and quantitative means—to show the numbers and use them to tell the story.

- Know how to apply an iterative approach. Community programs are not "fire and forget"—they need to be monitored and adjusted to continue growing in the proper manner.

Part of the point of having active community management through dedicated resources is to explore and potentially innovate. Failure may always be an option but you will never know if a new and innovative program or approach will work and succeed if you do not try. No one wins or loses a game in the first inning—so taking an iterative approach and experimenting is natural and often very rewarding in community management.

In line with these principles, these are some of the tried and proven community management tactics and activities that our team at CA Technologies leverages in their day-to-day activities.

Community managers should use these tactics:

- Create awareness of and promote the community to both internal and external audiences.

- Manage and act as advisors to the community board officers who lead the community (in our case—customers and partners).

- Create and deliver regular communications to the membership about activities or key content.

- Post regularly to external social channels (LinkedIn, Twitter, Google+, and Facebook) about activity taking place within the communities.

- Arrange and host webcasts—generally on a quarterly or monthly basis.

- Encourage and make arrangements for regular blog posting.

- Solicit content from internal teams and external community members.

- Upload and update content on the community site.

- Provide support to members on use of the site/associated technology.

- Facilitate conversations within the message boards.

- Test new features and functions and break/fix updates prior to launching into the environment.

You'll have to see what works for your community. We, in our approach to community management, have chosen to go à la carte with our offerings for each community we manage, so as to keep building based on the business goals and needs of the community while allowing for continual growth and increased interaction. Each community is mapped out along these activities, so that when each activity achieves success, another can be rolled out to keep the members engaged and deliver value back to the business, solve customer engagement challenges, and create continual feedback loops at the speed of social media and technology.

Why Communities Fail

Why do some communities fail? It could be as simple as the community was never meant to be and was predicated on the false premise of an audience, a need, or business outcome that was fabricated because people just think "community" is the answer without understanding the investment in time, money, and soul to achieve the transparency needed for success. Or it could be that that the balance between the system and the program was not met. Or the community may have served its purpose and is no longer needed. Or online interaction could have became vitiated by reflexive discord.

Reasons Communities Fail

There are lessons to be learned from each case where a community closes its doors, so let's look at a few examples:

- Community Focused around an un-engaging or uninteresting topic or incorrect audience

- Lack of dedicated community management efforts

- Unclear mission, purpose, goals, and measurements that lead to a lack of support

- Lack of content creation/community participation

- A technology platform that does not support the community needs

- Too much competition for the time and attention of the audience

- The business need for the community ends

This is by no means a comprehensive list—We're sure there are many other reasons that can be listed here, as the demise of every community is a bit different. But these are among the top reasons.

Community Focused Around an Uninteresting Topic or Incorrect Audience

It can be easy to develop content that is not right for the audience you are speaking to if you have not aligned the mission and purpose of the community with business needs correctly from the start. Divergence in the desired end-state creates tremendous discord and is the beginning of the end for a B2B community. A good example would be trying to overtly market goods and services to community members who are already customers—outright selling to those who have already been sold to delivers little value to either side in many cases.

Lack of Dedicated Community Management Efforts

The example mentioned at the start of this chapter documented by Tom Humbarger explains this failing point rather well. Counting on random, unguided participation by the membership and the employees and other subject matter experts may work if there is significant interest and natural collaboration. This rarely happens spontaneously, however, and should not be counted on for a path to success. In Humbarger's case, recall that when active community management was removed, page views, visits, and length of stay all decreased while the bounce rate increased. The community languished after a successful run with an engaged community manager and directed, focused efforts. Without dedicated community management, it is almost impossible to understand the value that is being created by the community—even if the community is seen as active or successful, there may be no view into the business ROI because there are no resources to manage it and measure it.

Unclear Mission, Purpose, Goals, and Measurements

Fact or fiction? The need for the *right* analytics in community management is more important than having measurements in the first place. Fact: If you have crafted a proper mission and understand the purpose of why you are developing a community and why you are investing in human capital to achieve certain goals, then the proper measurements become clearer. However, if any of these elements is not predetermined or clear in conception or definition, success will almost definitely take longer to achieve and the community may not last beyond the initial stages. This is due primarily to the fact that without the proper structure and measurements, the executive sponsorship and funding will almost certainly diminish and may end outright given the lack of value proposition for the company or customers. Community managers need to focus on two very important points here: the value proposition for members/customers, in order to keep them coming back; and—even more importantly—participating. Foremost, though, they need to find a way to define proper metrics and ROI and define the narrative back to executives that the effort and expense has direct relationship to both cost avoidance and revenue generation. It can be easy to justify the need for the "spend" on community from a qualitative perspective, but very difficult to do so from a quantitative one.

Lack of Content—Nothing to Interact On

For years, the communities at CA Technologies were left to interact among themselves. That had been the model for success when they operated as relatively independent regional user groups who met in person or on listservs.

As the model became more challenging to support, and given the unscalable nature of a global program managed from a central location in North America, an informed decision was made. We made the adjustment to transition to online communities so as to create economies of scale—and achieve greater cooperation by communicating essential information to our community members and customer base more efficiently. This saved on time, resources, travel expenses, and the like—and allowed us to impact a larger audience for less money and in less time than with traditional in-person meetings. It was the need for communication in between the face-to-face meetings that drove our move to online community, something we would venture was a prevailing thought given the additional penalties in time, effort, and expenses to attend these in-person meetings regularly.

When we moved from one format to another, one thing became immediately clear—we, as the vendor, were missing from the conversation. While engaged with the community leaders and members, we were not contributing enough to the conversation and were counting only on the external folks to keep the party going. Interaction was not building quickly enough, and once we jumped into the conversation and started content initiatives across support, product management, and development, interaction spiked and has been climbing high and to the right ever since. This proactive participation has also allowed for the company to help drive the conversation to where the company is going (such as product roadmaps, etc.) instead of where it's been. There is information garnered in the interaction in message boards, ideation, and webcasts that can be proactively incorporated into ongoing, future plans (especially with regard to agile development) because it is what is being worked on at the current timeframe rather than what has been left to the side for business or other reasons.

Technology Platform Does Not Support Community Needs

As social media/online collaboration has been changing, we have seen something similar within some of the communities we have worked with and managed over the years. Technology is a large part of the foundation of online interaction, and it never takes a break from evolving either. The two progress together and, hand in hand, push each other to new ways of interacting and new concepts of community. So communities sometimes find that they need to change the technology they leverage for their interaction.

I find it interesting that when I see discussions about technology that is dead or dying, it is presenting this as an end to community. The technology itself is an enabler of community, but not the reason for community itself, and a community with a good base will survive and adapt to new means of communicating with each other if needed. Some good examples are message boards and/or RSS feeds; both have been heralded as dead methods of communicating. However, both exist in large numbers and enable a massive amount of collaboration and contain voluminous amounts of information as repositories for online communities to reference.

New technology does not necessarily proclaim the death of a community, but perhaps signals a new way for the community members to contribute content and collaborate. If we step back to the days of the VAX and BBS systems, we would not necessarily be able to comprehend video sharing on a mass level such as we see with YouTube. Yet it has become a mainstream means of collaboration and has not yet brought about the demise of primary communication channels in online communities—the webcast, the web conference, or message boards—all of which were present capabilities during the VAX and BBS days of yesteryear.

The Business Need for the Community Ends

The last point about the business need ending brings up an interesting example. What the world saw as failure, the company saw as "the end of an experiment." Hyatt launched Yattit.com in 2008 as a place to capture the rise of online interaction and allow for travelers to share their experiences and interactions with the brand. The community lived a relatively short life of 19 months but was one of the first in the travel industry to tap into a company's loyalty program and bring that interaction online basically by acting as a virtual concierge. The surprise in the end was with how fast and unexpectedly they took the site down. In a conversation with Barbara De Lollis of *USA Today Travel*, a representative from Hyatt stated that the site was an iterative experiment and while it could be deemed a success, there were other opportunities in the evolving social media landscape which they might be able to leverage better.[12]

We may not know the underlying real reasons for taking the community down, but it does show worthwhile experimentation and follows the basic premise of innovation—fail early and fail often. In this sense, failure is not a bad thing and provides the necessary experience to come up with new innovative approaches and adapt to the ever changing environment of online interaction and collaboration.

An important takeaway is that many communities do come to an end and sometimes that end is seen as failure. The thing to focus on is that not all failures are bad, and there are many lessons to be learned during the postmortem examination of a community that closes its doors.

Summary

Here are some of the key concepts from this chapter:

- Find as many of the traits of successful community managers in your candidates as you can.

- Successful communities are usually the result of a broad team effort.

---

[12]Barbara De Lollis. "Exclusive: Hyatt Hotels closes its first social media web site as landscape evolves." *USA Today*, Accessed June 24, 2013. Available at: http://travel.usatoday.com/hotels/post/2009/11/exclusive-hyatt-hotels-closes-its-first-social-media-web-site-as-landscape-evolves/8427/1.

- Leverage the established principles of community management—but plan to add to the list based on earned experience.

- Address potential pitfalls early for a positive turnaround.

- Communities are not "fire and forget" projects—learn from the failures of your team and others and leverage those experiences for positive outcomes in the future.

As discussed in the first chapter of this book, people want inherently to be social and engage around areas that interest them—and most "community minded" people want to help each other to get their fix of dopamine and oxytocin. What enables this for your company is a person or team who can connect the business with the customers, find and corral content of interest, maintain a steady pace of interaction within the community, and leverage the outcomes, both quantifiable and anecdotal, to show the value derived from the investment in social capital. The three pillars driving these activities are reach, resonance, and relevance. This investment in the human side of social capital translates into monetary value by increasing trust, which translates to an increase in the speed of which business is done and lowering the cost of doing business overall.

Case Study in Focus: CA Technologies

As community managers, we are often asked: "Why does community matter? And why is it important that there's an online community for my product?"[1] There are lots of ways to frame responses to these two questions, but at the end of the day the answer to the first question is that your customers are people. It's important to remember that people are hardwired to be social. Our brains are set up to be rewarded for finding new information, receiving praise, bonding with others, and building up trust between people. As discussed in Chapter 1, the neurotransmitters dopamine and oxytocin in our brains help create and reinforce a sense of belonging and help drive us to have new interactions.

The answer to the second question is that our customers are already out there using social systems—almost everyone we know is already on LinkedIn and has a Facebook page. Glance at Twitter and you'll see a fire-hose gush of information about any topic you can imagine. When we talk about our products and how they relate to social networks, the thing to remember is that your customers are already on these networks and they are discussing their problems—problems that your products could help them solve. They are already using their own social networks and their own personal networks

---

[1]This chapter is loosely based on a talk by Sam Creek: "SocialU: A Sense of Community" (March 7 2013). www.youtube.com/watch?v=LpZTsN3wxXs&feature=youtu.be

of colleagues and trusted friends to talk about what they are doing personally and professionally, what problems they are facing, and what products they are using. We want to be engaged in that discussion but, more than that, we want to maintain and help guide that discussion. That is why it is important for you to have your own online community for your product.

▨ Why Does Community Matter for Your Product?

Humans are social. By nature, we live and work within communities.

We are already using it every day. Think LinkedIn, Facebook, Twitter, Google+, etc.

Your customers are using it. They are asking their networks about your products.

In the Beginning It Was Confusion

We started looking at CA Technologies' online community situation in 2008, as a follow-up to our work in consolidating and connecting the more than 300 regional user groups around the globe, so as to focus community efforts, aggregate activity, and better leverage and increase exposure of resources supporting the communities.

CA Technologies has a long history with user groups and other communities. Some started as far back as 1980 as user groups communicating with listservs and who met in person once a year at the CA headquarters. Others sprang up over time. Still others came to us through acquisitions. By 2008 there were at least eight different sites that users needed to go to when they interacted directly with CA online—as well as numerous other burgeoning online sites beyond the firewall offering community technology. There had been a product support forum, but when we looked at it, the last post was from 2005 and it simply asked, "Is anybody here?" Some of the acquisitions had brought along their own forums, which were independent and still active. CA partners were sent to a specific partner portal. CA Support had portals that maintained issues, a knowledge base, and downloads. There was a marketing site for information about our products, a separate education site, and various others dotting the internet ocean, each one an isolated island.

Each of these sites had a different look and feel. Each one required users to create a new profile, and there was nothing connecting all of this information about our customers together for our business. Some of the sites had overlapping functionality, yet each disconnected site had its own disconnected team of admins, developers, testers, and content providers moving on its own development schedule.

A Social Suite Solution

What we wanted to do was to bring all of these together and create a single user experience for our customer and partners that was consistent and brought them together with CA Technologies as a brand. We wanted to give our customers access to all the information they needed about our products in one place.

Where do you start? One of the most important problems to solve was the management of all of these identities. We needed single sign-on between the online properties. Bringing that together with a consistent look and feel allows the user to move across the online sites immersed in a coherent user experience. The different sites should be invisible to the user. For example, moving from a product page on the marketing site to the related community should be a seamless transition, and the controls and behavior should be consistent. Moving across should not seem like jumping between systems but between web pages of the same system.

For the community platform itself, we needed something that could easily provide the main social functions such as forums, profile pages, and blogs. We wanted it to be easy to configure rather than needing to be continually developed. It was important to us that it be interoperable. We wanted to be able to take a message board from a community and place it on the marketing web page or even into the product user interface itself. We also needed something that would be scalable and flexible as the communities matured.

At this time in 2008, a small company called Facebook had just begun accepting users who were not in college, Google+ did not exist, the first iPad had not been released, and the Apple App Store was just being launched. One thing that we did know is that these sorts of disruptive technologies were a given, and we wanted to make sure that the platform we chose would be flexible enough to accommodate them.

The Solution   A social suite that offered:

- Single sign-on among all web properties

- A coherent user experience across functions

- Interoperability with other platforms and services

- Scalability as the activity and membership grows

- Flexibility to accommodate the fast pace of disruptive technology changes

---

After researching the various solutions we narrowed them down to a few of the market leaders in the space and eventually chose an open-source, standards-based solution. Five months after choosing the platform we were ready to launch the first version during our industry convention, CA World, in May of 2010.

Listening to Our Users

Since then we have been listening and collaborating with our users to improve their overall experience by coming to grips with what we owned and how best to serve our community leaders and memberships. Right off the bat we started a collaborative community with our community leaders to let them give us feedback about where they wanted to see the communities go. Then we created one for the general membership to provide feedback about the system, MyCA, and the teams and programs that support the communities within the community experience.

Our first change was to update the UI and respond quickly to some changes that were needed to make the look smoother and more modern. We've continued that process to this day as trends in web design shift. We had made the decision to have our communities be customer-led, which means that each community elects a board of officers and we in turn grant those officers permissions to be administrators and moderators for their own communities. We worked with those officers to create a vision about where they wanted to take the online communities. What was going to be valuable to them and their members? This provided the foundation for our strategy going forward.

■ **Advice**   The best path to resolution for a problem encountered jointly may be to work together with both internal and external stakeholders in a collaborative fashion toward a joint solution.

Our first foray into research projects was to start an effort we called the Community of Tomorrow. We spent three months working with an active board from one of the more successful communities. We connected them with various teams and lines of business within the company to foster open collaborative discussions about the community and best practices for collaboration. We identified several ingredients of the community's success, as well as pitfalls the community had encountered and overcome. The output from this effort helped us move toward ensuring our communities are ingrained in the day-to-day work functions of as many teams within the company as possible—whether through the provisioning of content, direct contact and collaboration in webcasts and other content channels, or the solicitation of feedback from the membership.

Next we implemented ideas, using a product from CA called Idea Vision that was built on the Force.com platform from Salesforce.com. We integrated the idea function into the community sites. Each community that is enabled with ideas has a page that users can navigate to and submit ideas about product enhancements. They can also view other users' ideas and vote those ideas up or down. They can discuss the idea and refine it with their peers. CA Product Management reviews the ideas to see where they fit into the roadmap and then either accept or reject them and update their status accordingly.

These changes are then communicated out to the community. This ability to crowdsource and peer review ideas is a powerful model to assist our product managers to prioritize what comes next in our products.

Mary Greening, Principal of Community Management at CA Technologies, aptly describes the benefits of community to product development and adoption:

> *A strong software product community is a great resource for members to connect and share knowledge with other product users. It is also an excellent resource for companies that want to build best-in-class products. Smart companies can leverage community members in a variety of ways throughout the product lifecycle. Communities can be a great venue for crowdsourcing ideas and innovation during the research and development phase. Communities provide a rich pool of users for beta testing activities. Once a product is released, marketing and product management have a ready audience to evaluate new features and functionality. As the product matures, product management can build a trusted relationship with a community that can be used to introduce new products and services. Even as a product reaches end-of-life, a community can be a great place to facilitate that transition by showing users of an older solution the benefits of a newer one.*

One of the lessons that we learned during our first foray into the forums is that the communities are organic social entities that progress in regular cycles. They like having a schedule, especially when it comes to content. When you can get them used to expecting new content at regular intervals, you can observe the uptick in activity throughout the community. To capitalize on this we began working with our technical support teams to create a program we call *Tip Tuesdays*. One member of each support team heads out to his or her related product community forum and posts a tip or trick about the product in a specific Tip Tuesday category. It might be a solution to a common issue people are having, or it might show users undocumented features that will make their lives easier. We discovered that these Tip Tuesday posts began getting a lot of page views. The community leaders and our community management team broadcast these posts out over social channels like Twitter and LinkedIn, leading users to return to the communities pages to view these tips. This has been an extremely successful model and one that we are cloning for other business areas.

Supporting Our Users

By June of 2011 we were ready to upgrade our platform to the latest version at that time, increasing its capabilities and addressing some growing pains. This is a periodic process that we plan as the technical landscape of the social networking world changes and innovates. Our users ask for the innovations as soon as they become available elsewhere. For example, a few weeks after

Google+ launched, users wanted to know when we would have circles available for their contacts. It is an interesting balance for our customers: there are, on the one hand, those who can't wait for the next thing; and, on the other hand, there are plenty of others who don't want anything to change and are happy with the way things have worked for the last ten years.

As part of the upgrade to the platform, we began to integrate other customer-facing functions into the same user experience. The first area we added was support. We wanted users to be able to ask their peers a question, and if it was not answered, to be able to jump easily to support to open a support ticket. They could seamlessly navigate over to see updates, download patches, access documentation, and do other self-service tasks.

After support we integrated the partner portal. Rather than having our partners maintain two identities, one in the communities and another on a separate partner portal, they could log into one place and access discussions around the products as well as access partner-related material to help enable them selling and assisting our customers.

As we were doing these integrations, we learned that a lot of our users were putting code snippets out into the forums. This is a natural thing to see occurring in technical forums: samples of code, scripts, queries, and so forth are abundant. We were concerned, however, because this is a bit of a legal gray area. We want users to extend our products but we also want to make sure that anyone who was using code they found on the forums to understand the risks and that the code was not officially coming from CA. We began working with our users and our internal legal department to create the proper legal disclaimers to protect both CA and the users. We posted these disclaimers in all of the areas where code was being posted.

This was huge for our users and for the communities since we were able to promote this activity and drive valuable engagement. This helped extend our products and deeply integrate them into our customer's environments. This is the first step towards creating a marketplace for our users to be able to share or sell their add-ons to CA products.

Motivating Our Users

Most recently we have been creating a reward-and-motivation system based on a gamification platform. Our platform, like most online communities or forums, had a concept of levels in the forums based on activity. Within a forum a user will start off as a new member and then progress through the various ranks as he or she answers questions and performs other actions. We wanted to take that concept of leveling up through the forums and apply it to the entire site. We wanted the level of engagement and encouragement in the forums to be a part of every aspect of the site from blogs to wikis to connecting with other users.

Our first badging system was built to spread those behaviors across the site and reward specific groups of behaviors to become experts in particular tasks such as becoming a connector or a blogger. This successfully drove engagement. We saw answers to questions on the message board increase by 52% and discussions around blog posts increase by 600%. The users wanted more, though. They wanted it to be community-specific and to track more actions and provide more rewards. Based on this feedback, we re-launched the system nine months later, and this time we focused in on a set of levels per community. The goal in the new system is to surface experts in each community and to be able to see the relative standings between communities. For example, I could be a novice or a level one in the Infrastructure Management Community but a level six or Hero in the Application Performance Management Community. Other users can see these levels next to my avatar and this lets them know what my expertise level is with that product.

▨ **Note**   The CA Champions Rewards and Recognition Program:

- Focuses on missions for each community

- Guides users to the next desirable activity

- Tracks and rewards behavior for community members

Gamification has become a buzzword but it is really about paying attention to the customers and extending ways to reward and encourage their loyalty. For us, gamification is not about people winning prizes but about using a set of tools derived from game design to drive specific desired behaviors on the site. Our goal is to motivate our users to participate and provide a sense of momentum that will carry them from achievement to achievement and by doing so provide a meaningful experience with CA. Our community becomes more than a destination; it becomes a journey for our users to learn, use, and excel at our products. The outcome of that journey: increased customer loyalty.

▨ **Tip**   Gamification:

- Is a way of using user engagement techniques derived from game-design such as levels, rewards, missions, and contests to drive desired behavior for players or groups of players.

- Validates active participation (motivation).

- Has specific goals for the players to complete (momentum).

- Must provide a context for benefits (meaning).

How has all of this affected the growth and health of our communities? We began at our launch with nearly as many communities as we have today but with around 20,000 members. That number grew to nearly 100,000 members in 3 years. In addition to a nearly 40% increase in memberships across communities year over year, activity blossomed across the communities. In 2012, we saw near-triple-digit percentage increases, and the number of posts and blogs increased 60%.

Some of the most important metrics reflect improved relations between the community membership and the company itself. The number of positive ratings for content has increased more than 400% in the past year, indicating that members are finding content that is worthwhile and valuable. With regard to the value derived by the company, the number of posts marked as "accepted solutions" increased by more than 200% during 2012— which translates into savings through direct and indirect call deflection and cost avoidance. As with all start-up or entrepreneurial efforts, the percentages were extremely high in the beginning as we went from zero and built from the ground up. These are the numbers three years into the mission – and the goal is to keep the charts moving up and to the right through collaborative content and engagement initiatives.

How MyCA Is Structured

MyCA itself is broken down into two types of sites or collections of pages: there are profile sites for users and community sites for the communities. The community sites are made up of a number of subpages. You arrive at each community at the welcome page (Figure 6-1), which consists of introductory content, a calendar of events, a membership directory, and a leader board of the top users on the site. Typically a community will also have pages for forums, blogs, documents, wikis, and an administration page for the community leaders. Communities can also create specialized pages for other tasks such as surveys, polls, and other functions.

Each user has a user homepage (Figure 6-2). The idea is roughly similar to the profile page in Facebook. It has a place to provide a user description. CA is very careful not to reveal personally identifying information and all users are identified by their screen names, but beyond that they are free to give out more information about themselves. There are fields for their Twitter handles and their public LinkedIn profiles. This is also where they can track their progress through the levels of expertise in the various communities. They can also connect and follow other uses in the site. There is a stream of activities from the users they follow and the communities they belong to where they can click over to a user (who), or a post (what), or the community it was posted in (where).

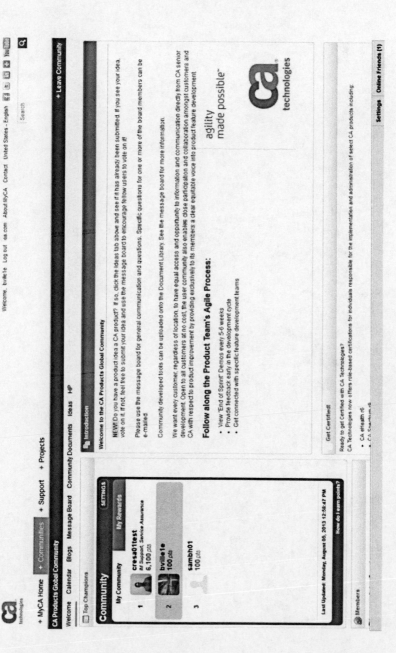

Figure 6-1. An example of a community landing page

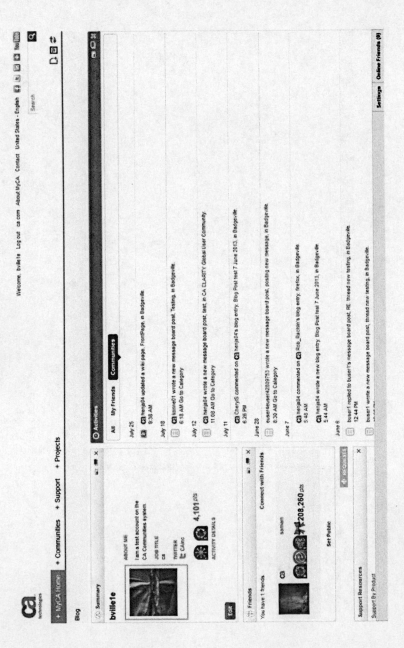

Figure 6-2. An example of a user page

We've been working towards creating active communities by aligning our business goals around the products with the goals our community members. We have a technical audience that wants to learn more about the products, get answers to problems they are having with the product but also to contribute back to the community either for their own status or for the good of the community. We want to increase the opportunity for that participation. To address that, most of the content areas can be subscribed to via RSS (Real Simple Syndication) or by e-mail and users can respond directly to the e-mail rather than logging in to answer.

Social sharing is another activity that we are rewarding our users for doing. We are badging them when they share content out to their networks on Facebook, LinkedIn, Twitter, Reddit, or hundreds of other sites. We see an increase in page views whenever we see content being shared in these channels.

We have begun engaging new members in a mentor program where our community managers provide monthly new member webcasts and introduce the new users to the site and to their peers.

Most importantly, we are working toward getting all of the technical users inside CA who design, create, service, and support the products to be connected with the technical users of those products. We want to build a collaborative development process where the customer becomes a partner as we work together to evolve the product to suit the market's needs.

The rewards and badging system also serves to identify the rock stars in our communities. We have found that the reward system has encouraged activity across the board but that it has turned our former rock stars into super heroes. We have some users who we think no longer sleep and appear to be answering questions 24/7. We want to find the passionate people and reward them for everything they are doing so they get the recognition that they deserve.

■ **Advice**   In addition to continually examining and learning about what you are managing, you need to learn to balance what you and your customers want against what is possible either in terms of the technology or available resources.

The Community Engagement Model

For this to work we have zones of influence that spread out from our team at CA to our community members. The CA Community team is small and has two main roles. On the one hand, they act as advisors to the community leaders and ambassadors for the communities to the internal business units. On the other, they manage and administer the system and plan for the next stage for collaboration. The next zone is comprised of our active employees and internal stakeholders such as product support and product management. Next are our community leaders, the dedicated customers and partners who have stepped up and volunteered their time to help run the community sites. The last and most important zone is made up of the community members, without whom the communities would not exist.

Learning about Our Membership

At the beginning of this chapter we mentioned the Community of Tomorrow project with our community leaders. The outcomes to that project made us think about other ways that we could begin to gain insight into the communities and, by doing so, improve on the communities. We reached out to a few academic institutions and become involved in some research projects that allowed them to look at information we had gathered from our communities. One of the first projects was with the University of Toronto and it involved a survey to our community members to determine where the community fell in a community maturity model. We learned a lot about our membership. One of the first things we learned is that e-mail is still king. Even with the prevalence of instant message and other social networks, users rely on e-mail more than on any other form of communication by a wide margin.

We found that our users were split down the middle between those who visited once a month or more and those who visited less than once a month. The ones who visited more often were more engaged, participated more, and indicated that they got more value out of the communities.

When we looked at the social networks that people were using one thing that jumped out is that YouTube was as prevalent as LinkedIn. It turns out that YouTube was a major source of content for how-tos, examples, demonstrations, and knowledge in general for our users. This is something that we have broadcast across the organization for other teams to capitalize on.

In regard to personally identifying information, our team was often asked, "What about LinkedIn? They say what company I work for!" But it's important to recognize that all of that info is volunteered by their users and encouraged by some game dynamics. We surveyed our users about this. We found that our users were split between wanting to remain anonymous and wanting to have all of their information public. There are a lot of security professionals on the CA communities and they were very happy with having a screen name and an avatar and being essentially anonymous. Others wanted to know whom they were interacting with. When they asked a question, they wanted to know if they were getting an answer from a peer, from a competitor, or from a CA partner. This is where we have basically compromised in having screen names and avatars but allowing the users to add more personal information if they want.

Measuring Success

Analytics based on the community population and activity has increasingly become a focus for the team. Table 6-1 shows the categories of community metrics that we have been reporting regularly to track how healthy the system is community by community. We began to extend that into call defection measurements to demonstrate return on investment. Account managers began promoting communities to customers and we began to measure the success of that outreach by tracking the percentage of their accounts that are now members. To address ad hoc queries coming from various business units about various aspects of the population and participation, a self-service reporting system was created. Most recently we have begun data-mining the conversations on the message boards to understand what topic areas are occurring and match that against our existing knowledge base and documentation to discover where we have gaps.

Table 6-1. Categories of Community Health Metrics

Registered User Population	Metric
Total Membership	Count
Distinct Members	Count
Membership Loss	Count (%)
Active Members	Count
Posters	Count
Authors	Count
Commenters	Count
Content And Interaction	
Threads Authored	Count
Threads Active	Count
Thread Responses	Count (%)
Thread Where First Response is from CA	Count (%)
Posts	Count
Avg. Time To First Response Across Threads/Blog	
Average Time to First Response Across Threads and Blogs	Count in Minutes
Total Blogs	Count
Blog Comments	Count
Solution	Count
Cost Avoidance - Call Defection (Direct)	Cost in Dollars
Kudos Received	Count

The biggest impact of all on our community transformation has been with the users themselves. When this project began the relationship between CA and the user group leaders was in shambles. For various historical reasons a great deal of distrust had grown between the community leaders and CA. The development of the online communities created an opportunity for CA to repair those relationships by reaching out and working with the community leaders and members. By demonstrating that we were listening to them and by following through with our commitments to them, we have not just provided a growing and healthy platform for collaboration, but we have also turned an antagonistic relationship into a mutually supportive one.

Summary

The way we often refer to our success in transforming regional user groups into online communities is by analogy to the NASA space program: We have, at this point, put a monkey into space. We have succeeded in proving that online community works for our company in our complex and challenging environment and structure. We consider what successes we have fleeting and that the real work is really only beginning, no matter how great or large our achievements have been to date.

In review of what we've discussed in our self-examination:

- Simplify the entire online experience. Your members will appreciate this tremendously.

- Collaborate with your leaders/stakeholders as often as possible, but strike outright to set proper expectations of timeframes, capabilities, resources, and technical limitations. You will then get better feedback and your transparency will build trust.

- Your content and your efforts should all be positioned with as much transparency as possibly, and mark as much content and material for public consumption as possible. It will help the company appear transparent, but it will help the customers even more in obtaining information necessary for their success.

- Gamification works, but only if you couch it in terms of the business and community. It needs to be transparent and just work for both sides.

- Continually research what you own, who you work with, and whether or not your efforts are having an impact on the business and are for the mutual benefit of the company and the membership alike. This balance is essential for the community to continue to mature.

- If you haven't established relationships with academic institutions to conduct your research, you are missing out on a significant opportunity.

So we will continue to venture forth and, while leveraging the established best practices of community management across this industry and others, we will continually look to the future to find new paths to success and work towards identifying a way to leapfrog the competition through collaboration with the people with whom we partner for success.

Business Impact through Community

Your online community is more than the sum of its parts. By engaging your customers in an evolving conversation about your products and their uses, you are involving them as a part of the product creation process and effectively making them partners in your business. The dynamic changes from broadcast and transactional to one that is relationship based. By listening and responding to customers, it becomes clear that the customers are your brand.

All of these statements sound great, don't they? They are all lofty ideas about how communities can help you. But, at the end of the day, what exactly should you be doing with communities, and what results should you be expecting? What are the tactics and methods for turning customers into partners? What do you measure to know if you are succeeding? What justification do you have to ask for resources to monitor a forum?

In the previous chapters we examined all the effort that goes into designing, managing, and maintaining a community. Now we will look at the impacts of those community-focused efforts on the company overall.

This chapter provides specific information about the areas of a business that can be improved or affected by communities. The business outcomes will depend on the primary focus of the community. Some communities are built around product or service support and are focused on either company-to-user interaction or peer-to-peer support, where your customers help each other. Other communities are focused on what the end users of a product can do to extend or customize the product. Still others focus on thought leadership, where the focus is on strategy in the marketplace related to the product. These communities can drive advocacy around the product segment and can be mined for market research.

Here are some real-world examples of community focus:

- *Customer Support.* VMware communities encourage their support personnel as well as their other expert community members who could be customers or partners to answer customer questions: communities.vmware.com/community/vmtn/.

- *Peer-to-Peer.* Apple support forums encourage peer-to-peer interaction and reward users who frequently contribute high-quality information: discussions.apple.com/index.jspa.

- *Modification and Development.* The Arduino micro-controller forums feature projects, how-to guides, and suggestions for using the Arduino system in a wide variety of applications from autonomous solar charging mobile robots to cocktail-mixing robots: arduino.cc/forum/.

- *Thought Leadership.* Smart Enterprise focuses on conversations between CIOs about best practices for IT organizations: smartenterpriseexchange.com/index.jspa.

The exact business outcomes you are looking for will be related to the functions of your online community. For example, a support-focused forum could be set up in a question-and-answer format, in which users can pose questions and then choose the best response. A development community could use ideas posted and voted on by the community to discover new features that would benefit the community at large or help guide the product roadmap. A thought-leadership community could rely on blogs from lead developers or C-level executives.

The sections of this chapter discuss several different potential outcomes and how the outcome can impact the business. Each outcome is broken into these subsections:

What It Means

What Functions Are Related

How Business Is Impacted

Notable Examples

How to Measure

We divide the outcomes into two kinds: direct and indirect. Direct business outcomes correspond to specific measurable actions in the community. For example, if you are measuring answers in a message board to show cost containment by deflecting support calls and if you assume that each question is a potential support call, then you can measure directly the savings for each answer as being the equivalent of the cost of the support call it replaced.

Indirect outcomes have a serendipitous correlation to your business goals. Let's look at the indirect benefits of posting answers in the example in the previous paragraph. Because the answer can now be found by other users with the same problem it may serve to deflect even more support calls. One way to measure that would be to look at the page views that the answer receives. Though we can't know for sure that every view corresponds to deflecting a support call we can assume an indirect benefit based on the amount of views that the answer gets. Let's consider the amount of views to be the popularity of the answer. Then the answer has an indirect benefit that is measured by how popular it is. It is indirect because we are assuming that a percentage of these views led to deflecting support calls as well.

To tie this together, an answer can be considered to have a direct benefit by deflecting a support call and an indirect benefit by potentially deflecting more support calls based on the amount of views that it receives.

Let's begin by looking deeper at a number of business outcomes and how communities relate to them directly.

Reducing Customer Services Costs

Reducing customer service costs can be accomplished in a number of ways: support personnel answering questions on a forum; peer-to-peer support where members of the community pitch in and answer each others' questions; or publishing and promoting documentation and technical articles to the community. Answering questions in a public forum or at least in a forum that is accessible by more than one user moves the question-and-answer process from a one-to-one value chain to a one-to-many value chain. Each answer that is provided may potentially answer a large number of customer queries, and this frees up your resources to concentrate on new problems instead of answering the same questions over and over. One of the key ways to drive peer-to-peer support is the use of notification and subscription systems. The goal will be to allow your power-users to subscribe to the forums so they are immediately notified when new questions come in and can log in and answer them. Subscriptions and notifications are also useful for when you want to broadcast new content or prompt your community members to assist with questions that remain unanswered.

Message Boards

Some message boards can be configured to display a question-and-answer format. This is a convenient way to track when a problem has been solved. Typically the poster selects if he wants the post to be a question and then selects the reply that comes closest to answering his question. Combining this with the ability for other readers to give posts a positive rating, or for them to mark that the answer helped them, can make calculating both direct and indirect case deflection easier.

Blogs

Posting important alerts, how-to's, and other technical articles can serve to deflect calls. To be most effective, blogs should have the ability to be subscribed via Really Simple Syndication (RSS) or e-mail notifications. Allowing posts to be rated and commented on gives the posts weight based on value and can uncover useful additional information.

E-mail Newsletters and Subscriptions (RSS)

Your customers won't always have time to check the forums for the latest information. Aggregating content into groups such as top posts, highest-rated posts, and the most-viewed answers in a given period and then sending that out to subscribers provides a convenient way for your customers to benefit from the activity on the forums on their own time.

Social Network Engagement

It's important to speak to your customers where they live. Your users may already be involved in social channels such as Twitter and Facebook as well as forums on other platforms such as LinkedIn, Stack Overflow, and Google+. Engaging them there provides a low-cost platform for customer support. These systems are already providing the infrastructure for mobile access, content rating, and notifications.

How Business Is Impacted

Reducing customer services costs is perhaps the most direct and well-known business impact from online communities. Each solution that your customers find in a public forum can be counted as an issue that did not have to come through your case management system and did not require the effort of a support representative to solve. Reducing customer service costs or support call deflection is commonly used to justify the return on investments for technology and staffing for online communities and social engagement. But the service or support organizations are not the only business units that benefit from this process. Marketing and customer success groups can discover potential case studies and surface product evangelists. Engineering or product development can engage directly with the customers to understand the customer needs directly. Documentation and knowledge base systems can be improved based on highly rated posts or answers that have helped other users.

Notable Examples Stack Overflow (stackoverflow.com/) is a popular public site for technical coding forums a question-and-answer format.

Quora (www.quora.com/) is based on the question-and-answer format and crowd-sourced answers from its members.

How to Measure Call Deflection

There are a variety of formulas for measuring call deflection, ranging from simple to complex. Here are a few examples, beginning with a complex one.

TSIA Method

The Technology Services Industry Association (TSIA) has published its take on call deflection, which requires a few extra measurements to be collected:[1]

$$R_E = \frac{V_C R_{SSF}}{V_{SS}(1 - R_S)}$$

Where

R_E = the percentage of people who would escalate from self-service

R_{SSF} = the percentage of people in the support center who tried self-service first

R_S = the percentage of people who were successful in self-service

V_C = total cases opened

V_{SS} = total self-service sessions

---

[1]Francoise Tourniaire and David Kay. Collective Wisdom: Transforming Support with Knowledge. HDI, 2006. www.dbkay.com/files/DBKay-SimpleTechniquesforEstimatingCallDeflection.pdf

If the escalation rate and self-service sessions are known, then

$$Deflection = V_{SS} R_S R_E$$

If only the answer to the "Did you try self-service first?" in the support center is known, then

$$Deflection = \frac{V_C R_{SSF} R_S}{(1 - R_S)}$$

This method requires a number of answers from surveys of your customers to establish the values for R_E, R_{SSF}, and R_S. One way of establishing that is to add a survey at the end of your self-service issue process when an issue has been resolved. The survey should ask questions to help establish if the user opened the case directly or if she attempted to find the answer through the online community.

Petouhoff Method

A method that does not require surveys comes from Forrester analyst Dr. Natalie Petouhoff:[2]

> Direct Deflection
>
> $S = Q \times A$ and $D = S \times R$ and $S = D \times C$
>
> Indirect Deflection
>
> $I = T \times R$ and $S = I \times C$
>
> where
>
> S = no. of new questions answered by superusers
>
> Q = no. of questions
>
> A = % of questions answered by superusers
>
> D = deflected calls
>
> R = industry call deflection rate (typically 10%)
>
> S = savings during the period
>
> C = cost of an average support call

---

[2] Natalie L. Petouhoff. "The ROI of Online Customer Service Communities: A Total Economic Impact Analysis Uncovers Big Benefits from Social Technologies." Forrester Research, June 30, 2009. www.lithium.com/pdfs/whitepapers/Forrester-ROI-Online-Support-Communities_s3NR5PeZ.pdf

Simplest Method

Monitoring and measuring page views, user visits, user-selected answers, post ratings, and user surveys all assist in determining the cost deflection for peer-to-peer support directly. There is an indirect component for users who are getting help from the answers or posts but are not interacting; it can be traced as a percentage of views, ratings, visits, or a combination of those.

The simplest and most direct method for tracking the cost savings from your community deflecting support calls is:[3]

$$S = (A \times C) - O$$

where

S = savings

A = answers

C = cost of an average support call

O = operating costs

For example, if savings are being tracked for a year, and there have been 1200 answers that year with an average cost per support call of $100 and the online community budget was $100,000, then:

$1200 \times 100 - 100,000 = \$20,000$

The net return on the investment for the community was $20,000.

▓ **Caution**   The biggest challenge may be finding the accurate cost of a case or issue for your company or the industry.

Crowdsourcing Product Enhancement Ideas

Ideation describes the practice of crowdsourcing ideas from your community and allowing users to vote on the ideas supplied from the other users. Typically, this is accomplished by allowing users to post their own suggestions or "ideas"

---

[3]Rachel Happe, personal communication to authors.

and then having other users vote those ideas up or down. The company then approves or rejects the idea based in part on the community feedback but also on other internal considerations and then communicates back to the community whether the idea will be part of the roadmap or has been rejected.

Communication, frequent feedback, and follow-through are key to the success of any ideation program. The company representatives responsible for ideation need to be engaged with the users, providing status updates and commenting in the idea discussions in a timely manner.

Ideas

Using crowdsourced ideas as a social tool or function is relatively new. There are several systems that provide an ideation tool and they are all relatively similar. Figure 7-1 illustrates the common features: allowing the community members to post, allowing the community members to vote, and providing the status of the idea (e.g., "accepted," "rejected," or "under review").

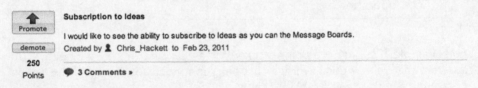

Figure 7-1. Ideas functions allow any member to vote and allow the other members to discuss the idea and vote it up or down

Message Board

Message boards can be used to gather product enhancement ideas from the conversations. Specific categories or boards can be set up such that the first post is an idea that the other members can vote up or down and then reply to the post and provide more discussion around it. Much like the question-and-answer format discussed earlier, some message boards allow posts to be marked with an idea status.

Blogs

By allowing any user to post a blog entry and by allowing voting from the other users, blogs can be used much in the same way as an ideas style system.

How Business Is Impacted

There are numerous advantages of a public ideation system for product management teams. It streamlines the enhancement request queue by allowing customers to see that others have the same request and they can vote that idea up instead of opening a duplicate enhancement request. Product management can use the vote tallies to help determine the priority and value of the enhancement to the larger customer set. The discussions around the idea can serve to clarify and improve the idea before it goes through the requirements process. The discussions can help the QA teams find the potential use cases for the proposed feature.

A note of caution here: For ideation to be successful, engagement and communication from product management will be required throughout the process. If product management is not fully engaged and communicating with the voters, then the company runs the risk of sowing disillusionment about its processes, products, and brand. That is not to say that ideation product management is to be ruled to the whim of the crowd—if, for example, an unrealistic request is voted to the top. Instead, product management need to be trained to understand that this is their opportunity to explain why they would not be adding that feature in such a way as to address it once and for all. The open nature of the tool should be seen as an opportunity to manage expectations in a transparent one-to-many way.

■ **Notable Examples of Ideation**   Dell's IdeaStorm (www.ideastorm.com/) allows anyone to suggest improvements to its products.

Starbucks (mystarbucksidea.force.com/) provides a similar service and crowdsources ideas about what their customers would like to see improved with Starbucks products and services.

How to Measure Ideation

Most ideation functions will have reports set up to pull the top-rated ideas or sort the ideas based on status. They usually will report on the lowest rated ideas as well. Other useful metrics include reporting on the amount of comments or the views an idea has received. Both of those are indicators of a popular idea.

It is important to report on the trends for status changes. Are the ideas being addressed only after a certain amount of votes? Are they being addressed in a timely manner?

Though these measurements can help an organization improve its process around ideation, they do not answer the significant business questions—namely, do the ideas that are crowdsourced and implemented help create better products and increase our sales more than feature ideas that would have been generated traditionally through personal vision and direct customer requests? Depending on your product and the maturity of the product in its market segment, the popular ideas that are generated from the crowd will fall into two main groups: the large sweeping ideas that are game changing and the specific ideas for incremental improvement. For a mature product, it is the second category that will yield the greatest gains. Ideation will serve in this case to root out corner cases and provide a poll across the user base as to how pervasive the issue is. The goal in that case will be the incremental improvement of the product quality based on the perceived benefit across the user base. The respective popularity of these incremental changes can help determine the priority in the order in which they are implemented. It is important to communicate to your customers that their input is valuable but it is one consideration that will be part of product management's decision. This may be an area where speaking with your legal department will be helpful to craft a set of terms and agreements around the ideas to protect the company in the case of perceived commitments.

▨ **Tip**   Give the company reps visibility. Put faces and bios behind the people setting statuses and give them the freedom to comment as individuals rather than with canned responses.

Incorporating User Data into a Social CRM

Online communities provide an opportunity to let your customers tell you about themselves. During the registration process and by maintaining and updating their profiles, customers will be adding information that will be useful to them, to other users, and to your customer information database. Incorporating this information into your existing *customer relationship management* (CRM) system will provide a more complete picture of who your customers are, what roles they play, and what is important to them. This means that you need to think through the registration and profile information very carefully before launching your system. Asking the questions upfront about what you want to know about your customers and how your users will want to identify themselves will help you design the appropriate system.

This also relates to your responsibility for this information. What are the legal ramifications of your customers knowing each others' identities? How can you protect their personal information? How can you ensure that they can be properly removed from the system when they desire to leave? Will deleted users impact your data integrity by leaving gaps in conversations? Do you want to enforce a pseudonym for each user or allow anonymous posting? Answers to these questions will impact your customer information policies and processes.

Registration Process

For your customers to join your online community they will need to register. At this point you can capture very specific information about the users: names, addresses, companies, titles, and so forth. You may need to capture contract information that proves that they are customers or partners. You may want to capture their preferences about what products they use. You may want to ask them about what industry they work in. When you put together this list of possible elements about a user consider what is required and what will be optional. A good litmus test is to ask yourself what you will do with the data and who in your company will be using it. Having too many required fields sets the bar too high for customers and results in having fewer users go through the registration process to join your site.

▨ **Tip** Social identities are becoming more prominent across new applications. Large numbers of your users will already have an ID on a system like Twitter, Facebook, or Google. Those companies provide application programming interfaces (APIs) that will allow you to leverage those identities rather than having to create your own registration process. This is beneficial to a customer since she does not need to create and maintain another profile on your site. However, this may not give you the detailed information you may want about the customer.

Profiles

After a user goes through the registration process, he will have a profile on your site that he can update with a new postal or e-mail address. This is also where you can allow users to provide additional information about themselves and customize their identities, for example, by allowing them to choose an image to represent themselves as an avatar. To capture more information after a registration with few required fields there is a technique called a "progressive profile" in which users are encouraged to provide more details about themselves to complete their profile. Many users will be familiar with this technique from LinkedIn, where a percentage of profile completion is displayed on the user homepages and hints and suggestions of what to add next are displayed on the page. You can use this technique to guide users to provide the information that is most beneficial to you.

Ranking

Many systems will track the likes or ratings that users will earn when they contribute content. Others are more complex systems that can track various behaviors a user performs and provides points for the user to accumulate. These points allow users to attain various ranks to show that they are experts in the system. Ranking systems can contribute to the social CRM by helping the system identify the experts and power-users in your community.

Badging

Alongside ranking systems, some sophisticated platforms provide badges or rewards that indicate that a user has performed a certain task or is a certified expert. Taken together with ranking, they are typically used as the foundation for a gamification system. Gamification systems can serve to motivate your community members, encourage desirable behavior, and provide meaningful context to their effort and contributions on the site. Gamification can also lead to users gaming the system by finding easy or repeatable ways of gaining points, which can have serious ramifications for programs with tangible rewards. Many sophisticated online gamification platforms contain anti-gaming mechanisms such as limiting how often a behavior can be rewarded or how many times a day the reward can be given. It is important to understand and implement these features to avoid the risk of some users abusing the system if given the opportunity.

Personalization

There are several different paths to user personalization. Some systems grant users the freedom to choose what their site looks like and how it behaves, such as a customized theme in Tumblr. There are other systems that learn from user behavior and provide users recommended content that suits them. In either case the business can learn what the user is interested in and can use that knowledge to improve its communication with that user. Personalization can also be used to provide some of this information back to the user to help her to understand the level of her interaction with the site. Common statics for social sites will show a user how many posts she has made, when she first joined and last logged in, or how many connections she has.

How Business Is Impacted

The more you know about your customers, the more you can tailor your products and services to meet their needs. Additional profile and registration information will allow you to understand what role the community member plays in relation to your product. This can help you serve the right information to the right people at the right time: technical information to technicians, strategic information to executives, and so forth. For smaller companies, personalization can give insights into where your customers spend their time on your site and allow you to focus more efforts in those areas. In either case the business goal will be to provide the user with rich information about your products and services in relation to their role. By providing this context to the user rather than having the user browse and search through your site to find it, you can help to lower the customer service cost and shorten the sales cycle.

■ **Tip**　As more personal information about users surfaces through various social channels it's important to remember not to be too invasive. Using personal post content to foster business communications such as mentioning users' recent vacation pictures on Twitter may seem too invasive to customers and may have negative consequences in your business relationship. When you are acquiring detailed personal information it's important to remember: don't be creepy.

■ **Notable Examples of Social CRM**　Salesforce.com (`www.salesforce.com/`) leads the way as a social CRM and accommodates extending customer profiles with their social identities.

Foursquare (`foursquare.com/`) is a location-based service that allows you to discover recommended businesses around you. The system encourages you to check into these locations and by doing so earn various badges of your achievements.

How to Measure Social Data in a CRM System

The registration information you collect should provide the baseline of useful information for your users. If possible, this should be aligned or synchronized with your CRM system to provide the most accurate and up-to-date information about your customers to all members of your organization. For ranking and badging, reporting systems and leaderboards will allow you to track your customers' progress and find influential users and community experts.

Let's look more deeply at a number of business outcomes and how communities relate to them indirectly.

Customer Retention and Customer Loyalty

Customer retention and loyalty is the likelihood that the customer will remain with your product and continue to purchase that product or service and maybe also recommend it to others. It can be measured in a number of ways: customer satisfaction, net promoter scores, and so forth. Essentially you want to find out how satisfied the customer is with your product or service, how likely he is to buy again, and how likely he is to promote your product or service to someone else.

Any area that is thriving—in other words, that has a lot of activity, views, or visitors—is likely to be an area indicating customer satisfaction. Of course, context matters. If people are having issues with your product, being very active by posting about it may detract from their overall estimation of your company. Off-topic or tangential conversations can impact the value of looking at activity, although that can be mitigated somewhat if you provide an avenue for those conversations in such a way that you can easily filter those areas from your reporting.

Surveys

Surveying customers about their satisfaction and likelihood of recommending your product or service is the most direct way of measuring customer satisfaction. Be careful not to over-survey your customers or the survey spam may serve to impact negatively their estimation of your brand. Think about how often you fill in surveys for services you use. There is a fine line to tread. To lessen the burden of the surveys, rely on community leaders to help be the voice of the customer. However, the occasional broad survey helps keep the community voice heard for all and not just for the vocal minority. It is also important to remember that people are not always truthful or accurate when they are reporting about their own actions, so it is helpful to compare survey answers against the numbers that are found by tracking the customers who actively promote your company through social channels, referrals, and case studies.

How Business Is Impacted

A positive community experience can drive customer satisfaction and the likelihood purchasers will buy again or promote your brand. This can indirectly impact revenue by increasing new sales and renewals and extending your market reach.

■ **Notable Example**   Satmetrix Systems provides a Net Promoter Score (www.netpromoter. com/why-net-promoter/know/) to track where your customers fall on a scale between promoters and detractors of your brand.

How to Measure

Surveys provide the clearest way to measure customer satisfaction. They are, however, not the only way to track the impact of online communities on customer retention and loyalty. If you have a system in place that is tracking user behaviors, then you will be able to track trends in the percentage of how many users return over various intervals (daily, weekly, or monthly). The user-generated content can also be analyzed by tools that check for sentiment. These tools search for specific terms that relate to a possible emotional sentiment for each post, such as *happy, enthusiastic, neutral, angry,* and *sad.* Analyzing sentiment has limitations. It cannot detect sarcasm, for example. It should be used to supplement other tools to give an overall picture.

Thought Leadership to Engage and Inform

Thought leadership gives the product and market experts inside your company a platform to reach your customers. It gives the customers insight into the products and services and the best practices around them. The intention of thought leadership is to show the market at large how and why your products or services are relevant. More importantly, demonstrating thought leadership reveals what the leaders within your company are thinking about and how that may relate to the customers. Thought leadership can be provided from the customer perspective as well. It can allow your top customers to tell their stories about how they used your products and services and provide testimonials about the benefits they have achieved.

Blogs

Blogs provide the most common channel for thought leadership. The format promotes a single idea at a time with related discussions and comments. Blogs accomplish a few tasks very well. They keep the audience focused on a specific topic. They are easy to promote and cross-promote with direct links to the post. These links can allow pingbacks that allow the post to be tracked as it shared across the Web. Most importantly, the authors of the blog give a personality to the company, giving it a more human touch rather than only presenting content from an impersonal marketing site.

▓ **Tip**   The success of blogs is dependent on fresh content being delivered at regular intervals. In this day and age of fire hoses of content coming from other social channels, blogs need to be the more interesting and deep, long-form elder statesmen of web communication in comparison to the short, fast bursts from Twitter and Facebook.

Message Boards

Thought leadership in message boards is trickier than the direct one idea at a time format of blogs. The most direct way to display thought leadership within a message board is to carve out a specific forum or category that is made to promote certain kinds of content. An example is a category that promotes pro tips about a product posted by members of the development and support organizations on a weekly basis. Coming from within the organization gives the posts a sense of authority and regularity so that the customers can expect new info in a specific timeframe and a familiar way to comment and discuss the content.

■ **Tip**   A popular event on message boards, the AMA or Ask Me Anything, provides live chats with thought leaders on a message board. The audience can ask questions and engage with the leaders in real time. First popularized by the news aggregate site Reddit, it has grown in popularity, with well-known actors and artists, scientific leaders, and even the president of the United States taking part.

Wikis

Although the real strength of wikis lies in the constant somewhat anonymous edits and revisions that improve the content, the original author of each page can be displayed on most systems, which, similarly to a blog post, provides a way of exhibiting a single idea from an authoritative source. The goal would be to have the community collaborate and help improve the content directly in the page, although in practice discussions and comments to the article are more common.

Newsletters

Newsletters fall into a very traditional format of displaying thought leadership. They are a collection of articles based around a topic or product and authored by experts within the company or guest authors and sent out at regular intervals. Traditionally these have been curated from within the company, and an editor who is an employee of your company selects the content. The newsletters are then formatted and e-mailed out to a list of subscribers maintained by a listserv. However, newer, more sophisticated systems tap into a preference-based model for both content and for frequency of delivery. This gives customers a customized view about your company that is delivered in the optimal manner for them to consume it.

How Business Is Impacted

Thought leadership promotes the leaders of your company as the subject-matter experts in their field and helps give your existing and potential customers ideas about ways that your products and services can be applied to them. These posts and articles should be promoted over social media channels with the goal that they be shared and reposted. This extends your company's visibility and market reach beyond just the visitors to your site. Your company wants to show that your leadership understands and anticipates trends in your industry. This leads to customers increasing their trust in your company about the company's direction. This trust can be key to purchasing decisions and can help sway the argument for renewing contracts or sticking with your products.

Notable Example   Smart Enterprise Exchange (smartenterpriseexchange.com/index.jspa) is an industry-focused thought leadership community for CIOs and other IT leaders.

How to Measure Thought Leadership

Measuring thought leadership veers more into the traditional models for measuring marketing reach. The sections below look at new tools that take advantage of social channels and sharing content. Some of these are free and others are pay services. Thought leadership events such as webinars can be used to track and cultivate leads based on attendance and sales conversions.

Views

The number of hits or views that a piece of content receives is a straightforward and simple way to determine its value by measuring its success and popularity. Simple view counters have been around since the early days of the web. These days, however, tools such as Google Analytics or Webtrends allow you to add a snippet of code to your site and then measure the traffic that is coming and going.

Visitors

Similarly unique and returning visitors can be measured with popular traffic analyzers such as Google Analytics and Webtrends. Measuring the new and returning visitors seems like a great way to measure the following that your thought leaders are building as they convert first-time viewers into loyal readers.

However, those numbers are becoming increasingly difficult to measure accurately with the rise of cookie-blocking tools such as Abine's DoNotTrackMe[4] and other privacy tools for browsers as well as other popular privacy measures that browser makers are beginning to build directly into their products.

---

[4]www.abine.com/dntdetail.php

Because the traffic analyzers rely on cookies to tell whether or not a user is visiting the first time, when they are blocked the visitor is either not counted at all or is always counted as a new visitor. Because views are not subject to this kind of blocking as they are based off of the actual http request for the page, they remain an accurate measurement.

Comments

A lively discussion around a provoking post is a solid endorsement that the thought leadership is making an impact. One way to measure that is to count the amount of comments being made about that post. This can be done in blogs by enabling comments and measuring their post count or, if the thought leadership posts are done in a message board, by counting the amount of responses in the message thread. These responses are generally considered to have more value even than page views and should be accorded a higher value when reporting the success of posts.

Ratings

Enabling a rating system on your blogs, message boards, or articles is another way of measuring the value that the content provides. There are many systems for this, with as many perspectives as to which system is the best. Some allow only positive ratings while others allow content to be voted up and down. Others display a range of values such as 1 to 5 stars that the user can vote on. Usually star rating systems also show what the user votes, as well as the count for how many votes have been cast and the average star rating drawn from the overall votes. Generally, unless your customers are curating your content (with systems such as Reddit or Slashdot), you will want to stick with positive ratings or rating values such as five-star ratings. It's important to be consistent with your ratings and to provide instant feedback.

Shares

Social networks thrive on sharing content the users find interesting. By tracking and measuring each time your content is shared, liked, commented on, or in any other way interacted with throughout the variety of social networks, you can measure the reach and impact your content has far beyond the visitors to your site.

To accomplish this, the first step is to make the content easy to share. Most social networks will provide code snippets that you can add to your page that make it simple for your users to click an icon and share out the content.

Twitter, Google+, Facebook, and LinkedIn all provide widgets to enable sharing for your content. There are systems like AddThis[5] that provide an easy way to manage sharing to multiple networks. Another way to track these shares is through URL shorteners such as bitly.[6] They shorten your URL to a manageable length for a status update or tweet but they also track what happens and who views this link because their system needs to be contacted to convert the short URL into the full URL.

There are also social listening tools such as Radian6[7] that scan multiple social networks for specific tags, words, or phrases related to your brand or product. These tools can alert you in real time when conversations are happening about your products or services. Social listening can be done within tools as well, for example, using the @name identifier in Twitter. When you hear stories about people tweeting how much they like Morton's steak as they board a plane to Chicago only to arrive and have a steak waiting for them at the airport, chances are the social media department at Morton's was using social listening to engage with that customer.[8]

Embracing a Culture of Transparency

A company's culture speaks volumes about the way it interacts with its customers. What do we mean by company culture? It's the pervasive norms and behaviors that imbue the interactions between the employees at all levels. For example, how tolerant is the company of its employees' personal expression? Is it OK with employee publicly questioning company policy? Until the advent of the Internet and, more recently, the resounding voice social networks gave to the customer, it was easy for a company to shield its culture from its customers or at least to pretend to.

In today's world, where a simple misstep can cause a massive outcry across multiple social networks, it behooves companies to understand the relationship between the way they operate and what the public expects of them. A culture of transparency and openness speaks to an honest relationship between the employees of the company and extends to its customers and partners. The goal of a culture of transparency is to build trust. Transparent cultures promote efficiency and good decision making by providing more insight into the needed information across the board.

---

[5]www.addthis.com/
[6]bitly.com/
[7]www.radian6.com/
[8]Graeme McMillan. "Man Uses Twitter to Get Free Morton's Steak Dinner Delivered to Airport." *Time*, August 23, 2011. techland.time.com/2011/08/23/man-uses-twitter-to-get-free-mortons-steak-dinner-delivered-to-airport/ (accessed June 29, 2013).

This is not a simple task and it requires making some tough decisions. More transparency and openness will bring up a number of difficult questions. Will being too open about your products leave you at a competitive disadvantage or will it help extend your foothold in the market by creating an ecosystem around your products? Openness and transparency do not have to mean that you pull the curtain aside to reveal completely the wizard working the controls but it can mean that your online communities could become a vehicle for honest discussion with your customers about problems and issues that they are having. In turn this can build goodwill and turn a dissatisfied customer into a brand evangelist.

Message Boards

A message board is the perfect vehicle for open discussions with your customers. Chances are if there are issues your customers will run into with your product, then the message board is where they will head to let you know. That also means that they are perfectly positioned to allow you to head off disgruntled customers and defuse a potentially damaging situation by posting to the boards when you find out about problems. The important thing is to engage and do so honestly. This means being tied into the conversations by actively monitoring or subscribing to the boards.

If your internal culture is not transparent, however, two or more employees may give customers conflicting information or there may be gaps in information that can end up on the message boards. This can lead to escalations and have ramifications for the employees who provided the information. It can be embarrassing for your company or potentially much more problematic. It is important to be clear about your internal policies on how to prevent dispensing conflicting information to your customers and how to correct it when it happens.

Blogs

Blog posts offer a great opportunity to alert users of an issue. Often blogs are used to promote and showcase success stories, and though that is important and has been covered in the section on thought leadership, one of the most interesting things a company blog can do is to lift the veil and reveal what really goes on during product development. Hearing about the failures, challenges, and hard work that goes into your products can create a sympathetic bond with your customers. Letting them know you tried features x, y, and z and that you found certain impacts and had to revert will show that you are listening and pushing the product. Giving your customers this privileged access into your process helps foster the sense that we are all in this together, interactively shaping the product.

Ideas

Earlier we discussed ideation and how crowdsourcing ideas can make an impact on your product direction. We emphasized that it is important to provide continuous feedback of the status of ideas. That is a perfect example of the culture of transparency in action. Continuous communication and status updates will keep your customers engaged and involved with the process. This in turn will increase the mutual value you and the customer will get out of the system.

Social Networks

In the previous section about thought leadership we discussed ways to track shares of content through social media and mentioned tools like Radian6 that not only allow you to listen into these channels but also to engage in real time. That engagement can be another opportunity to interact with your customers in an honest and straightforward manner in the social networks they are comfortable in. There are plenty of examples of how honest interactions in a social network can yield excellent results.[9]

How Business Is Impacted

Transparency and openness can impact your bottom line by instilling increased customer trust and loyalty. No one plans for a PR disaster, but practicing the habit of being open and transparent about your business processes can give you the advantage when it comes time to explain what happened to your customers. If you have already built up measurable trust with your customers then chances are they will give you the benefit of the doubt and hear you out. If you operate in a world of obfuscation and secrecy it will be more difficult institutionally to step forward and explain how a situation came to be without seeming culpable. The role of trust in business relationships has been thoroughly studied and there are several popular resources that go in depth into the steps to create trust between you and your customer.[10]

---

[9]Todd Wasserman. "Red Cross Does PR Disaster Recovery on Rogue Tweet." Mashable, February 16, 2011. mashable.com/2011/02/16/red-cross-tweet/
[10]David H. Maister, Charles H. Green, and Robert M. Galford. *The Trusted Advisor.* Free Press, 2000; Stephen M. R. Covey and Rebecca R. Merrill. *The SPEED of Trust: The One Thing That Changes Everything.* Free Press, 2008; David Horsager. *The Trust Edge: How Top Leaders Gain Faster Results, Deeper Relationships, and a Stronger Bottom Line.* Free Press, 2012; and Robert C. Solomon and Fernando Flores. *Building Trust: In Business, Politics, Relationships and Life.* Oxford University Press, 2003.

▒ **Notable Examples**   Red Hat: (www.redhat.com) and Zappos (www.zappos.com) have both been lauded for their leaders' open discussions of company matters over public social networks. This has led to greater trust from their employees and from their customers, who get the rare opportunity to see the behind-the-scenes decisions that affect the brand.[11]

How to Measure Cultural Transparency: Surveys

Asking your users directly about how much they trust your organization is the most straightforward way to measure the effectiveness of your open communication policies. This is very similar to using surveys for customer retention and customer loyalty that we spoke about earlier. Questions about how trustworthy your company is can be included in the same survey.

How to Measure Cultural Transparency: Sentiment

Measuring sentiment is relatively new. The concept is that the user-contributed content in message boards or related social channels such as Twitter referencing your brand is collected and analyzed by an algorithm. The algorithm catches certain phrases or words as being positive or negative in association with your brand. In this way sentiment analysis should tell you if users are saying positive or negative things about your brand and products.[12]

One problem with this approach is that it's hard enough for humans—far more an AI or simple context matching algorithm—to detect sarcasm and irony online. As Ben Zimmer put it: "One criticism of 'sentiment analysis,' as such research is known, is that it takes a naïve view of emotional states, assuming that personal moods can simply be divined from word selection. This might seem particularly perilous on a medium like Twitter, where sarcasm and other playful uses of language often subvert the surface meaning."[13]

[11]John Hall. "10 Leaders Who Aren't Afraid To Be Transparent." *Forbes*, August 27, 2012. www.forbes.com/sites/johnhall/2012/08/27/10-leaders-who-arent-afraid-to-be-transparent/ (accessed June 29, 2013).
[12]Maria Ogneva. "How Companies Can Use Sentiment Analysis to Improve Their Business." Mashable, April 19, 2010. mashable.com/2010/04/19/sentiment-analysis/ (accessed June 29, 2013).
[13]Ben Zimmer, "Twitterology: A New Science?" *New York Times*, October 30, 2011. www.nytimes.com/2011/10/30/opinion/sunday/twitterology-a-new-science.html?_r=3& (accessed June 29, 2013).

▓ **Tip** Intellectual property, compensation, contracts, and personally identifying information for your customers and your employees all have legal ramifications. When in doubt, err on the conservative side and speak to your lawyer or law department. Include your legal department as soon as possible to help create business practices and engagement models that allow for openness but don't threaten your business model.

Improving Social Business Maturity

The social business maturity model, as discussed in Chapter 3, refers to the progress an enterprise goes through toward integrating the collaborative aspects of social networking into their business processes. Companies are progressing from using social networks to broadcast marketing at customers to integrating social networks into daily activities in a collaborative effort to work with their customers in technical support, crowdsourcing of product ideas, and collaboration internally between business units. This could be seen as a meta-impact because it is the culmination of the other business impacts as it helps to move a company along the progression toward becoming a social business. A complete social business unites an internal fully networked social environment with its external social networking efforts.

Although the majority of the business would view this as a process, from the perspective of community managers or program owners, social business maturity is a business outcome because they are working toward evolving the systems so that they provide more value. In this sense, laying the foundation properly to enable progression through the stages of maturity will accelerate the process and deliver the proper outcomes that will provide benefits to the other business units.

Engagement in each of the social functions of the online community internally and externally as part of the operating process for each business unit is the ultimate goal of social business maturity.

How Business Is Impacted

Why is it important to mature into a social business? Will getting involved in an online argument over your product affect your shareholders?[14] Will missing a well-placed tweet have an impact on your bottom line?[15]

---

[14]R. L. Stollar. "Applebee's Overnight Social Media Meltdown: A Photo Essay." Word Press, February 2, 2013. rlstollar.wordpress.com/2013/02/02/applebees-overnight-social-media-meltdown-a-photo-essay/ (accessed June 29, 2013).
[15]Katherine Fung. "Oreo's Super Bowl Tweet: 'You Can Still Dunk in the Dark.'" *The Huffington Post*, February 4, 2013. www.huffingtonpost.com/2013/02/04/oreos-super-bowl-tweet-dunk-dark_n_2615333.html (accessed June 29, 2013).

In this day and age the answer to that is a resounding yes. Deb Lavoy points out seven ways to frame the answer:[16]

1. Communication is no longer hierarchical.

2. The opposite of social is fear.

3. Collaboration is the only path forward.

4. Collaboration promotes mutual value.

5. Collaboration exposes patterns that can be measured about your business.

6. The old funnel sales model is over.

7. It's not about understanding social; it's about understanding you.

Articles like this, and the work others are doing in examining the new business models, tend to reveal something powerful: the social business model is not replacing the old model; it is providing more insight into the way business has worked all along. New tools enabled faster communication, but in the end it is about relationships, your company's ethos, and customers trusting you and your products and finding mutual value on a transactional basis.

Numerous examples have been presented in this chapter of online communities having a direct impact on a brand. Moving the company along the progression of becoming a social business directly impacts your conversion rates from marketing, your net promoter score for customer experience, and your bottom line with increased revenues. Staying engaged and abreast of not only your brand but also its relevance to the overall culture can create a direct connection with your customer that was nearly impossible a decade ago. Not being engaged, on the other hand, will not mean that the conversation isn't taking place; rather it means that the conversation is taking place without you.

■ **Notable Example** Cisco (www.facebook.com/Cisco) has done an exceptional job creating a Facebook presence that reflects its multiple business units and goals as well as large product set.

---

[16]Deb Lavoy. "If Social Business Is the Answer, What Is the Question?" Product Four, March 7, 2012. productfour.wordpress.com/2012/03/07/if-social-business-is-the-answer-what-is-the-question/ (accessed June 29, 2013).

How to Measure

Several analyst groups have been creating models to measure the progression of social business development. The Altimeter group provides a questionnaire that companies can use to gauge where they currently are and where they should be going.[17] Modeling these styles of business isn't specifically geared toward one end game, but there are a variety of models that can work for your company. At the end of the day, the real goal is to understand your company is not working in a vacuum, that relationships and communication are key.

■ **Tip** Chances are other areas in your company are working toward the same goal. This is a perfect place for collaboration between business units to help the goals of each business unit as it pertains to the voice of the customer.

Summary

Your online community should be a vital part of your business strategy. Understanding what you want out of it, how you will measure it, and where you want it to lead to will impact several aspects of your brand, from building revenue pipelines to improving customers service and spreading information about your brand by word of mouth or tweet, as the case may be. Ignoring the online conversation about your brand will not make it go away and can end up creating a PR nightmare that can have serious negative impacts. Worse yet, asking for people to not talk about it can create the opposite effect.

Embracing and engaging with the online community can open up channels that traditionally took years to create in the old sales model. Here is a quick rundown of the direct and indirect business impacts that we have examined in this chapter:

Direct Impacts

- Customer services costs are reduced.
- Call deflection from peer-to-peer support created on your online community's message boards can show a measured impact on lowering your service costs.

---

[17]Jeremiah Owyang. "How Mature Is Your Company? Social Business Maturity Quiz." Altimeter Group, February 10, 2011. www.slideshare.net/jeremiah_owyang/how-mature-is-your-company-social-business-maturity-quiz (accessed June 29, 2013).

- Crowdsourcing of product enhancement ideas becomes possible.

- By providing an open and transparent way for customers to submit product ideas and to vote and comment on ideas submitted by others, greater insight can be gained about how and where your products can be improved to have the greatest impact.

- Data are provided to incorporate into a social CRM system.

Capturing more information about your customers allows you to understand their needs and improves your ability to communicate effectively with them on their terms. It helps you to build the products and services that address their needs.

Indirect Impacts

- Customer retention and customer loyalty are improved.

- Active collaboration with your customers elevates them to partners you are working with; this in turn increases their loyalty to your brand and products, leading to more purchases and renewals of services.

- Thought leadership engages and informs.

- By providing insight into why your products stand out, you improve your brand's standing overall in the marketplace.

- A culture of transparency is embraced.

- Openness and transparency build trust between your company and your customers, leading to stronger relationships and a better opinion overall about your brand.

- Social business maturity is improved.

Understanding where you are today and where you want to go will reveal insights into how your company relates to your customers and how those relationships can be improved. This in turn drives mutual value between your company and the marketplace.

We have discussed how each one of these business goals are enabled by specific functions of the online product communities and where these can be measured. But these are only a handful of examples. By understanding where you are as a developing social business, you will be able to uncover business goals and impacts specific to your situation and your customer segments. Opening the channels of communication will open the door for more opportunities. Your goal is to foster the community conversations that will improve your business. At the end of the day, it isn't important to tick a set of checkboxes that proves you're a social business just because you have team of interns tweeting marketing materials. Rather, *social* has to become second nature to your business processes. At that point it isn't even necessary anymore to use the adjective *social*. It's just *business*.

Developing B2B Social Communities

Measuring Community Business Returns

Measure twice, cut once.

Measuring a community's success brings us back to the maxim in Chapter 3: "Measure twice, cut once." You should always verify your measurements because, once you cut the raw material, there is no going back. Business decisions often work the same way. Once you launch a new or updated product, there are often no more opportunities for adjustments or fine-tuning. It either sinks or swims. In some cases it simply lands without any fanfare, which can be the same as sinking. After that initial launch, more measurements are usually taken, but they are lagging indicators. The post-launch measurements can monitor the trend and provide lessons for next time, but they often cannot be brought to bear on correcting the trajectory.

Where can businesses go to make measurements "before cutting"? They use surveys, focus groups, beta testers, and early adopters. Their online communities can provide a captive audience to engage in all of these methods. But what about customers' behavior in the community aside from the product launch? Is there insight to be gained by measuring the normal everyday interaction? What can that insight tell you about how to position a launch? What can it tell you about your customers, your market segment, and your raw material? How can you create a baseline off of which progress can be measured?

In Chapter 7 we covered various business impacts from social online communities and how to measure them. In this chapter we are going to dig more deeply into the measurement side. First we will cover the mechanics of online community measurements and analytics:

- What metrics are available
- How to deliver the news
- What tools can make this easier
- Pitfalls to avoid

Then we will circle back and look at how customer behavior metrics meet the needs of the business: how they lead back to the business impacts from online communities and forward to the decisions about fostering the communities. Those topics will include:

- Developing business goals from metrics
- Growing strategy

How to Be Valuable

Valuable, usable, and engaging: these are the qualities that successful online customer communities strive for.[1] But although all good community leaders within an organization hold these core values paramount, when business stakeholders start asking for hard ROI metrics, most community teams get a little nervous about how to prove value and define success. So, when the "What has the community done for me lately?" questions get asked, panic sets in. The result ends up being dashboards and spreadsheets and charts galore. Community managers send reports off to leadership with fingers crossed and a heavy heart because they know the data don't really tell the whole story. Often the timeframe is too short, or apples are being compared to oranges, or there isn't an industry standard to measure success against. But they don't know a better way to communicate the results that are available to them. Consequently, and not surprisingly, the documents submitted rarely satisfy leadership's key questions

- What is the value of the online community to the organization?
- What is the value of the online community to the customers?
- Are these values aligned and, if so, how and in what ways?

---

[1] This section, "How to Be Valuable," is adapted with permission from the following article: Vanessa DiMauro, "Designing Metrics for Online Communities," posted to *Leader Networks*, August 18, 2011. Available at www.leadernetworks.com/2011/08/designing-metrics-for-online-customer.html.

Number of members, number of new members, length of time on site, number of posts, top 100 content sources visited, and the varied array of measures counted are all important to some degree—but they rarely tell the real story. This is because those metrics are too far removed from the business strategy and member needs to be meaningful. So, community budgets are cut, the cost-center label is assigned to them, and staff is given additional responsibility within the core operations outside of the community because no one understands the value that community can bring or is bringing to the company.

This all-too-common tale of community woe will not be avoided even if you have a strong community to begin with and just have difficulty articulating the value. What organizations often forget is to align the business goals of the organization with the community operations. The real value of the community is often found by looking to business definitions of success and member definitions of success—determining where the community works in support of the larger business goals and customer needs, and then determining in what ways business goals and customer needs align (Figure 8-1).

Figure 8-1. Your community focus is the intersection between business goals and customer needs

Know What You Have to Know to Go Where You Want to Go

To pull this together you will need to start with understanding how your business measures success today. What are the strategic priorities? What are the operational metrics? Next, consider what your customers perceive success to be and how they want to be recognized. Then you will need to understand exactly what you have available to you in terms of metrics and other areas for measurement for your community. The intersection of these areas shown in Figure 8-2 captures the focus area for community metrics that support the business goals by following customer behavior.

Figure 8-2. The intersection describes the valid metrics for measuring customer behavior in the community that supports business goals

Once you have that understanding, you will need to learn how to collect the data and put them into a meaningful format that can be collected and updated. Steps will need to be taken to cleanse the data of unwanted elements (such as test posts that were done while testing the system during deploys). After you have verified the actual customer data that you will be collecting you can set up a baseline for your current state. At that point you will need to set a timeframe to collect consistent sets of data. Setting up the baseline will give you an idea about where you are and allow you to make the first projections about where you want to go.

These first goals shouldn't be set in stone; they are basically a shot in the dark. It isn't until after the next wave of data comes in that any trends will begin to make themselves known. The first two sets are a starting point, but again, they might be flukes. For example, if you begin your measurements for community activity in November and add December as your second set, chances are that those are not indicative of the yearly community activity because there are long holidays and personal distractions during those two months.

Patience is key. Communicating this to business stakeholders upfront is important to setting expectations. Knowing that proper analysis is coming after the first few intervals will also help you prepare by beginning to collect data at the earliest opportunity. There is one more important aspect to setting up the baseline, especially if the online community is new to your company and your customers. Capture from the current business metrics how problems are being solved before the community. Understand the process, costs, and measurement.

For example, if you are setting up a support community, then it is important to understand how customers are supported today, how that is measured, and what the costs associated with customer support are. Cases may be open on a one-on-one basis, and success is measured by the amount of same-day closures that occur. Each case may be estimated to cost $100. Understanding this is a fundamental aspect of your baseline, as it lays the foundation for how you will measure your success to compare the similar value that your community is now providing. In the example we have provided about the new support community, this means that the goal will be to provide a more efficient and cost-effective manner of support by providing peer-to-peer support and answering questions that benefit all the customers, rather than just the one who opened a case.

This Is Beginning to Sound Like Math

Before we launch into community metrics, let's cover a few basic skills that will be helpful in working with these numbers. For the most part, the formulas we are looking at will be basic formulas such as for averages and means that are available out-of-the-box in common office programs such as Excel. Every once in a while, it will be useful to understand a few concepts to apply them in the correct context.

Understanding the different ways to represent the average can help you choose the right one when you are looking at very small differences (mode), very large differences (mean), or huge differences (median) in values. When we say *average* we are looking for what the representative set or example is for a given set of data. Usually this is done by finding the arithmetic mean: adding up all of the values and then dividing by the number of values. However, that is not the only way to find an average value. You can also look at the *median*, the central value in a set of data ranked in order between the highest and lowest points. There is also the *mode*, which is the most frequently occurring value in a list of values. You might use all of these if you have outlier data that skew the mean—for example, a handful of power users who post thousands of times more than the normal user. In that case it represents your community better to look at the median for the average because it removes the impact of the outliers that can throw off the mean. The mean and the median are restricted to numbers, but the mode can be useful as well when you are looking at how often a non-numerical value is represented.

The other concept that is useful in providing an apple-to-apple comparison between different populations is the use of ratios. Ratios remove the absolute disparities between larger and smaller populations. For example, if a forum has only 100 users but has 100 posts a week, how does it really stack up to another forum that has 1000 users and 800 posts a week? Obviously the second forum has more people and more posts but does that mean it is really more active? By creating a ratio by dividing the posts by the population you can compare their relative activities. In this case we can see that the first forum has a ratio of 1.0 post per user per week (100 posts/100 users), whereas the second forum has a ratio of 0.8 post per user per week (800 posts/ 1000 users). So the first forum is one tenth the size of the second forum but one quarter more active.

Metrics

Data tend to be either feast or famine. Some systems have very little for you to go on, and what is there is difficult to extract from the user interface itself, or it requires add-ons and extra services to be really useful. Others will be able to display very granular sets of data per user. In the one case you can starve from the lack of quality and consistent information. On the other hand you can drown in the unrelenting stream of data. The goal is to find the sweet spot where the data that you are pulling is aligning to the business goals you have set for the communities as well as for your business. Let's cover a few of the common metrics that are available to online communities and drill down into what they mean and where they can be applied.

Views

View count or *page view* is a basic metric discussed in Chapter 7. Essentially, the view count clicks up by one for every view that a page gets from a user. Beneath the hood, the system is literally counting the page load requests from a visitor on a website.

View count can be used to track the relative popularity of content, such as the relative popularity of several sections of your site split among business units or products.

Visits

Visits count each unique IP that requests a page. Setting a cookie to recognize when a visitor enables new visitors to be distinguished from returning users. One visit may consist of one page view or many page views.

Visit counts for returning users can be used to track user retention, in other words how many of your visitors are returning visitors vs. new visitors. Visitor counts for new visitors can be used to track the reach of new content. In more sophisticated systems the path origin of the visitors can also be tracked. This is useful in tracking the success of *search engine optimization* (SEO) efforts. When optimized content is found through search engines such as Google, their path from their Google search to your site can be tracked as part of the visitor tracking.

Populations

User population may have any of several meanings. A user population may count visitors, registered users, or specific community members.

What you count will depend on the context of a given system and your metric purpose. For example, considering everyone who visits your community as a community member will greatly increase your population, but when you use your population in a ratio with a participation metric such as message board posts the wider definition of the population of community members will make your community seem less active. Taking into account granular attributes for your populations can help you slice and dice the lists you pull for specific purposes. For example, measuring intervals between login dates can help you find active vs. inactive users. Pulling their company information or addresses can help you find account coverage or regional populations.

■ **Tip** Population metrics can begin as an ad hoc request out of curiosity, but be prepared for any of those reports to become a scheduled report. It's a good idea to ask the requestor: If this report were needed on a regular basis, what would the frequency be? Treating ad hoc requests as if they are new regular reports will prevent one-off measurements that are difficult to reproduce.

Posts

A *post count* is the total number of posts that a given registered user or community of users has contributed to a given community platform—typically message boards, blogs, or comment sections to blogs or other pages. Beyond the actual count of the posts, knowing when the posts were made and where they were posted can end up being very helpful. This can be important in systems that consider all posts as part of a discussion and use metadata to separate out where the discussion is happening. Separating them into their specific areas is important because not all sections may have the same value to a community. Thought leadership communities may place more weight on their blogs and the discussions that occur around specific posts than on posts in other areas.

Post counts can be used to track activity by community, message board category, or by user. If you have a large number of communities, forums, or users, this is a metric that benefits from using ratios to compare the post counts of different populations if, for example, you are looking for the activity between multiple product communities.

Likes or Ratings

Likes or *ratings* are evaluations that users can give to content. There are a number of ways that these can be implemented, and each method affects the way that they can be measured. Some systems, such as Facebook's Like buttons, allow only positive evaluations. Comparing content with only likes appears at first to come down to a simple count. As with posts, however, if you have larger and smaller populations whose likes you need to compare you will need to reduce absolute counts to ratios of like counts to population size.

Ratings can also be implemented for binary positive or negative ratings. Comparisons in this case need to take into account both the net rating and the amount of votes given. For example, a piece of content that has 22 positive ratings and 2 negative ratings can be considered more highly rated than a piece of content that received 120 positive ratings and 100 negative ratings, even though both have the same net value of 20 positive ratings. The content piece is considered "active" or "controversial."

The other way that ratings can be implemented is a gradational value system, such as from one to five stars. Yelp is a good example of this sort of rating system. It is similar to the positive and negative rating system but builds in a concept of an average rating. It is useful in a value rating system to display the current average, the number of votes cast, and the ability to provide feedback to users to let them know what rating they chose for the content.

Seeing the voting trends over time helps the consumers of the content as well. If a piece of content is consistently getting positive ratings over time, it is more valuable than a piece of content whose initial positive ratings dropped off over time because it became stale or was found to be unsatisfactory for some other reason.

Ratings and likes can be used for a number of purposes. They disclose the value of the content in a system to the community, indicating whether it is popular, controversial, or not valuable. It can also reveal trends that show which content may be stale or out of date and should be reviewed. Each implementation will require the appropriate analysis depending on whether it is a value rating system or a system based on likes or positive ratings. Consider using a ratio with populations, views, or visitors metrics as a way of normalizing the results between differing sets.

Answers

An *answer* is a specific sort of post or reply that has been indicated as directly answering a question or as an indication from other users that the post or content has helped them by answering a question they had. One way of looking at answers is that they incorporate a very specific sort of rating into the feedback. Chapter 7 discussed how forums can be set up in a question-and-answer format. Content such as knowledge-base articles often include a button or area for users to click that states something like, "Did this item help you? Click here to let us know. Your feedback helps improve our content."

Answers and other user feedback mechanisms, such as "This helped me" buttons, can be used similarly to likes and ratings. The difference is that these mechanisms indicate a direct rather than a relative value. These methods can be overlaid on top of likes and ratings systems to help indicate direct and indirect value of content. For example, some knowledge-base systems will display both a star-rating system and a place that indicates that the knowledge-base article helped the reader. Sometimes answers are implemented as a privileged feature where only experts can provide the answer, conferring a degree of authority to the answer.

Surveys

Surveys provide a direct means of putting specific questions to your population. The value to be gained from most of the metrics covered in this chapter is based on inference from comparing numerical indices of user behavior and opinion over time or between populations. Surveys are a much more direct way of eliciting user answers to specific questions.

Certain items cannot be inferred from the metrics that follow user behavior. As explained in Chapter 7, formulas for determining things such as indirect cost deflection depend on understanding the percentage of users who have indicated that they were helped by content. This can be inferred from likes but it is a weak correlation that depends on other values such as views and visits as well. Surveys provide a very direct measurement of what a sample segment of the population thinks about your community and their satisfaction with the value it provides. It is worth noting that surveys do not replace the answer functionality even when they are asking about whether content helped a user. They are not focusing on specific content and its value but rather the larger impression the user has about the value of the community.

Polls

Polls are another direct means of getting information back from a community. Typically polls have very few questions—often just one. Polls ask a question and offer a few possible radio-button responses from which a user can select only one. Sometimes an accompanying chart shows the current or final results of the poll.

Polls are geared toward answering a specific question or set of questions at a time. They are less invasive than surveys inasmuch as they tend to ask fewer questions and take up less participant time; they also offer direct feedback of the results and so are much more likely to elicit a response. Polls offer a quick and easy method to take the social temperature of a community. Because they require little investment on the part of the user, they can be helpful early on in a community's life to help drive user engagement.

Text Mining

Text mining (also known as *content analysis*) provides a means to discover meaning from the data that are being collected as your users contribute content. These kinds of free-form data are referred to as unstructured data. By contrast, structured data consist of specific data types and have context bound to specific fields. For example, the name, company, telephone number, and address fields in a registration form collect structured data. Fields for telephone numbers and e-mail addresses are bound by data-type or valida-tion rules: a US telephone number requires ten digits; an e-mail requires an @ symbol and a period at some point in the suffix. The other fields may be free-form but they are contextual; the first name and last name fields have very specific meanings and they can be used for specific operations. For example, after you've entered your first (Dave) and last name (Thomas), the web application states "Welcome Dave" in the header.

Unstructured data, on the other hand, result from content items such as message board posts, where there is a subject, body, and attachments but users can enter anything they want. The context is not bound: the subject and body can be about anything. So how do you make sense of this free-form data? One way is to analyze the frequency of certain words or phrases across posts to discover context based on those terms. This can be done in one way in which the frequency of terms is discovered in clusters in any order (*support*); and another way in which the order of the words is counted as well (*confidence*). This is an example of association-rule learning.[2]

For example, finding clusters of terms such as *coffee, french,* and *press* can have a specific degree of support (number of times those terms are found together in any order) and confidence (number of times they occur in that order). The implication of the order of the terms is that *x, y,* and *z* often occur together, but chances are that when they occur in the order *x, y, z* it means something. Another way to put this is that the higher the confidence, the more often that having *x* and *y* implies *z*.

---

[2]K. Lai and N. Cerpa. "Support vs. Confidence in Association Rule Algorithms." In *Proceedings of the OPTIMA Conference,* October 10–12, 2001.

Data mining is a science unto itself. For communities, data mining can be used as a way to find important topics that the community cares about or identify off-topic conversations. It can be used to discover words that can be used in a tag library to help increase the relevance of posts and new content through search.

Reporting

After you have decided on what metrics make up your key performance indicators and you have set up a rhythm for when you will be pulling the data, you will need to decide how you will broadcast your findings. The means of delivery can be informed by the audience you are trying to update. Some methods are applicable for internal stakeholders who are making monthly or quarterly decisions about their goals. Others are perfect for high-impact one-shot snapshots of the current state of the communities. Some are geared for users who will need to act on the information and others are geared for executives who just need a quick health check.

Periodic Reports

Reports are usually spreadsheets of data that are pulled periodically. They should be consistent each time they are run. The content can be overwhelming, and there is a natural tendency to pull a superset of data and let the audience decide how to filter and sort it. The danger with that approach is that no two people will sort and filter the report the same way and the same superset can end up saying multiple things. It is worth your time to ask your audience what specifically they are looking for and gear each report to be the final word on that particular question. Your audience can help determine whether it is a dense operational report for community managers or a one-slide scorecard of strategic KPIs for executive-level decision makers.

Ad Hoc Reports

Even when you think you have all the data covered in your periodic reports there will still be new questions that require ad hoc reports. Again, the simplest approach is simply to pull a superset and let the audience figure out its answer. This can fast become a problem if the ad hoc report that you did not filter yourself becomes a required periodic report. It is best practice to treat ad hoc requests as potential new periodic reports. This will save you time and effort in the long run.

Charts

Charts provide a visual display of quantitative information. They can be useful to show

- Comparison between similar items over time or over a few variables

- Distributions and histograms

- Composition of an item over time or as a single snapshot

- Relationships between similar items with a single or multiple variables[3]

Figure 8-3 exemplifies a comparison chart showing the trend of posts in a forum over time.

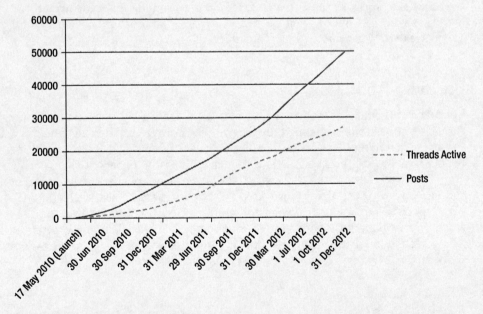

Figure 8-3. Chart displaying the trend of posts vs. active threads in the CA Communities

An example of a distribution chart is given in Figure 8-4, which plots the number of views against the number of posts in a thread.

---

[3]Andrew V. Abela. *Advanced Presentations by Design: Creating Communication That Drives Action*. Pfeiffer, 2008.

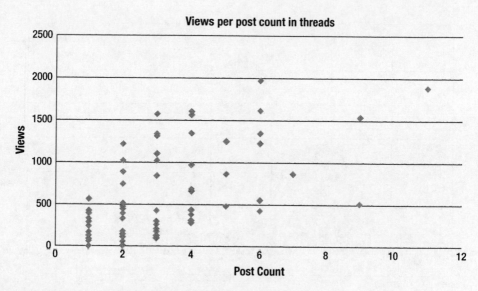

Figure 8-4. Chart displaying a scatterplot for views over posts

An example of a composition chart is given in Figure 8-5, which shows the distribution of answers across communities in a pie chart.

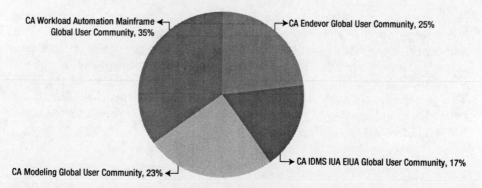

Figure 8-5. A composition chart of answers provided to questions in the forums across CA product user communities

An example of a relationship chart is Figure 8-6, a bubble chart showing ratings from users as proportionately sized bubbles arrayed as a function of post count over time.

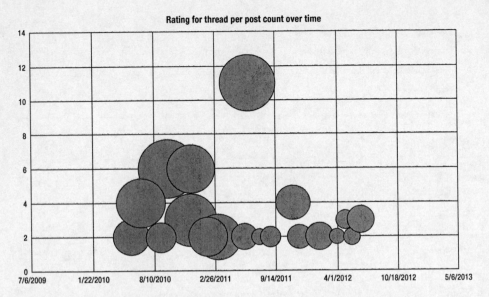

Figure 8-6. A bubble chart showing ratings for threads per post count over time

Infographics

Infographics are time-honored communication devices that are becoming increasingly popular and easy to create. Typically they marry several charts and other displays of data to represent a story about a particular topic. Often the infographic emphasizes a particular point of view through the use of the visual metaphors rather than providing a neutral presentation of the data. The venerable ancestry of infographics is exemplified by the 1869 chart reproduced in Figure 8-7, but new web-based tools have made it much easier for the layperson to create infographics.

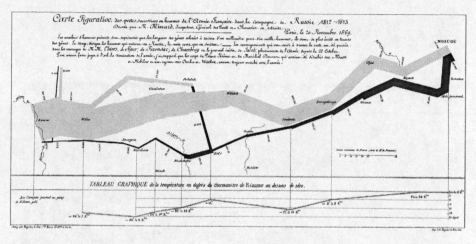

Figure 8-7. Charles Minard's famous infograph published in 1869 depicting Napoleon's ill-fated invasion of Russia by displaying the population of the army as it marched to Russia and then retreated after defeat

Infographics are useful for representing interrelated concepts within a common context. Stacking data, such as using geographic representation filtered by demographics, is a particularly engaging infographic device.

Dashboards

Dashboards are interactive charts that allow a viewer either to observe the effects of changing variables or to drill down to different levels of granularity. They are used to provide a snapshot of key performance indicators and display patterns and trends to the user. Often the audiences for dashboards are executives or administrators who can use the immediate feedback to be alerted of anomalies (Figure 8-8).

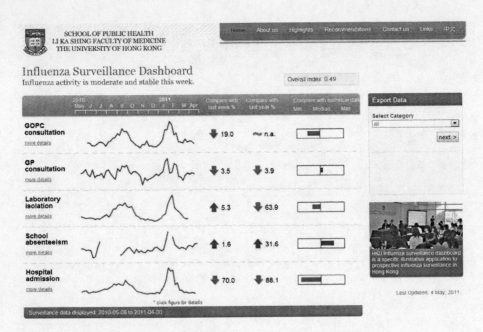

Figure 8-8. A sample dashboard built to monitor influenza outbreaks[4]

Tools

We list below the most common tools for reporting community metrics but, given that the industry is constantly moving and evolving, think of the examples below as guides rather than prescriptions. The goal in this section is to familiarize you with what is available and how to select the tools appropriate for different purposes. The intention is not give you a list of must-have items. Each tool has strengths and weaknesses, and some are appropriate for only large enterprises and would be overkill for small businesses. We describe each tool, identify its appropriate use, and supply examples of enterprise-ready tools and free alternatives where available.

Spreadsheets

The most common tool for analytics is the humble spreadsheet. Columns and rows of data, formulas, and pivot tables are one of the most common ways information is communicated throughout offices all over the world.

---

[4]Calvin K. Y. Cheng, K. M. Dennis, Benjamin J. Cowling, Lai Ming Ho, Gabriel M. Leung, Eric H. Y. Lau. "Digital Dashboard Design Using Multiple Data Streams for Disease Surveillance with Influenza Surveillance as an Example." www.jmir.org/2011/4/e85/

Familiarizing yourself with the basics of using spreadsheets will go a long way to enabling your ability to report against your data. Sorting, grouping, formulas, macros, and pivot tables will be essential to your analytics toolbox.

The most common spreadsheet is Microsoft Excel. There are traditional competitors from IBM's Lotus and from Apple in the form of the Mac OS X app Numbers. Google offers one free to users, as well as an enterprise cloud-based version for a fee, that is the simply named the Spreadsheet part of the Google Drive suite. Depending on what kind of shop you work at, one of these is likely at your disposal.

Databases

Spreadsheets are great for capturing a lot of related data but they quickly run into limitations when you are moving beyond simple formulas and pivot tables. Pulling data from several sheets based on a unique user ID is impossible, as are complex conversions of the data or filters based on criteria from multiple sheets. When these limitations begin to crop up it is usually time to begin using a reporting database. Relational databases provide multiple tables of columns and rows that can be joined based on common fields. Complex queries can be written that pull data together from multiple tables and present it in the desired format and sorting. Typically these are written in the database query language or *structure query language* (SQL). Results from database queries are usually either counts of specific groups or lists of data with associated information.

Your database reporting choices will typically be tied to your community platform of choice. If your system uses MS-SQL you could report directly from there or from a reporting clone.

Mashup Tools

Sometimes a single database is not enough. This is becoming increasingly common as modern systems begin using integrations with services to provide needed features. A common example for online communities would be reconciling data captured directly from your platform with data captured by Google Analytics about your site's traffic. You have common elements between the systems—a message board thread's URL, for example—but the systems are entirely disconnected. Your platform may be behind your firewall on a MySQL database and your monitoring tools may be in the cloud. At best you can run reports from both and use either your database or a third tool to bring those reports together.

That is where mashup tools come in. You may be familiar with mashups in the music genre, where one or more songs are blended together and the context is stretched in new and interesting ways. Business mashups are similar in that they take content from disparate sources and bring it together to provide a new perspective on the overall data. For example, you might combine the geographic distribution of your online community visitors with the geographic distribution of your sales contracts to discover that your customers are more global than your sales lead you to believe and your site needs more localized content.

There are two ways that mashup tools typically work. One set works by connecting to data sources directly with connections such as Open Database Connectivity (ODBC), or they import files from locations that are placed there by the other systems. Once they pull the data together, keys of common data are used to bring the information together in a way similar to how queries are pulled from multiple tables in a database. JackBe Presto is an example of the first type of mashup tool, importing and connecting to multiple data stores.[5]

The other set of mashup tools rely on APIs or web services that communicate to disparate systems and pull the data they need at the time and provide tools to filter and display the results. ProgrammableWeb is a popular example of a tool that can take public APIs and bring together the data to display how they relate in interesting and new ways.[6]

Enterprise Data Warehouses

There is another option that large organizations typically use and that is the data warehouse. The idea is similar to a mashup tool; all of the data are imported and normalized into the same large database and all of the reporting is done from there. The major difference here is that the enterprise data warehouse usually includes information from finance, sales, marketing, and customer support as well. This means that the data about your customers in the online product community can be closely aligned to what you know about them throughout your business. The benefit of this is that it allows having a more complete picture of your customer throughout their lifecycle from a potential customer through to user and hopefully a loyal brand advocate.

At the end of the day the enterprise data warehouse is just a database. This can be accomplished with MS-SQL or another enterprise level database such as Oracle.

Text Mining Tools

Getting the data into the right location to run queries against is half of the battle. Up until now we have been talking about tracking lists and counts—for

---

[5]www.jackbe.com/
[6]www.programmableweb.com

example, lists of members who belong to your community or your community member count. However, the online community is uniquely situated for users to generate content about your products. All of this content is unstructured data—which brings us back to data mining tools. As mentioned before, data mining has varying degrees of complexity. At the simplest layer is tracking frequency of phrases or words throughout the user contributions and finding clusters of related terms. More complex levels involve performing semantic analysis on the content and discovering overall positive or negative sentiment or generating recommended content based on the content of users' posts.

There are enterprise-level tools built around content analysis, such as HP's Autonomy.[7] Autonomy uses what HP calls an Intelligent Data Operating Layer (IDOL) to search and analyze any kind of unstructured data. The idea is that the search returns related results based on the semantic context. There are also free tools such as Rapid-I's RapidMiner.[8] This is an open-source tool for data mining content imported into it. It provides preprocessing, visualizing, and modeling of unstructured data.

Social Network Analysis

Because online communities are made up of users who are contributing, collaborating, and connecting, there is also the opportunity to mine the data around the user connections. This is referred to as social network analysis or social graphing. It can be useful for finding the power users or influencers in your community, as well as the up and coming potential leaders. By examining who follows whom or who responds to whom, you can begin to discover clusters of users that then can be mapped to particular topics, products, or roles.

Social graphing technologies are built into some online community platforms, such as Lithium.[9] For standalone analysis there are tools such as Gephi, an open-source data visualization tool suited for social network analysis.[10] NodeXL is another free tool that can work in conjunction with Excel reports.[11]

---

[7]www.autonomy.com/
[8]rapid-i.com/content/view/181/190/
[9]lithosphere.lithium.com/t5/science-of-social-blog/Social-Graphs-The-Art-and-the-Insights/ba-p/5713
[10]gephi.org/
[11]nodexl.codeplex.com/

Big Data

Big data is a term that refers to large data sets that can now be accumulated through new technologies for monitoring, sensing, and tracking. As interactions become increasingly made over wireless networks by mobile devices or using rich media such as VoIP or video, more metadata and relationships are being tracked and recorded. All of this data poses several problems around collection, storage, analysis, search, and other data mining. Your customers and their transactions on social networks, interactions with your products, or posts to your online community are all part of the massive data sets that are being generated. Wading into the big data pool may not be necessary for your business now, but big data seems to be taking the place of the mashup market and the enterprise data warehouse market, offering a way to understand your customers in a multitude of contextual layers. Big data is giving way to predictive analytics, in which a set of data about a user can successfully predict his or her likely next action or questions. The results from big data are affecting areas beyond where traditional analytics reached—far beyond marketing into the molding of content itself.

A number of new technologies are being created to analyze and visualize these large data sets. At the end of the day, they are designed to detect the same sorts of connections, clusters, relationships, lists, and counts as do the traditional tools we have already discussed—just on a very large scale.

Pitfalls

There are a few caveats to keep in mind when diving into the analytics for your community. The first is: *Just because you have the data doesn't mean they must be reported.* Drowning your audience in meaningless stats can have a negative impact by obscuring the true measurements of the worth of the community. Too many different stats can make it difficult to find real successes or hotspots that need attention. Providing too many options ends up providing distractions that can make it difficult to align data to business goals.

When asked for very specific data it is often tempting to pull a large superset of data and allow requestors to sort through and discover what they need. The danger in this is twofold: First, everyone can potentially sort and filter the data in their own way, so the data can be inconsistent if pulled from two different people. Second, as we have mentioned previously, any ad hoc report can potentially become a periodic report. Therefore it is worth the effort to work with the business to understand what result it is looking for at the end of the day and what the data will be used for. This will help frame the question or query and help set the context for the results. The metrics without the proper context can be interpreted incorrectly, and this can lead to poor or uninformed business decisions. Providing governance around what kind of reports are acceptable, which can be declined, and which can be escalated can also help keep the focus on business goals.

Another major pitfall is measuring apples against oranges. There are so many various values available that it can be easy to pull two together that may not be properly related and expect it to be representative. We have covered ratios as one method of working through this. It helps to keep in mind what the goal is of any comparison: Is it to set goals for growth, to discover the current health of the community, or to compare yourself to your overall market segment?

Developing Measurable Business Goals

Delving into metrics and analytics for your community is often kick-started when you are asked to justify the expenditure on the platform and to demonstrate a solid ROI. This happens when the community team is looking for executive advocates supporting their efforts. However, when the data have been collected and filtered it becomes clear that the analytics can serve a more important role as part of other interrelated efforts across the business. Measuring community growth as a return from marketing efforts or the cost savings from call deflection as a result of peer-to-peer support will have positive effects in business units across the company.

After the reports and ROI justification it is important to focus on two areas: first, where the analytics can help improve the system and community program; second, where it can tie into and support other business goals across the company. For the first area of focus, the same metrics that can help justify the system can serve as starting points to measure the success of the community. Understanding the baseline for the community and for the same process without the community is key, for measuring the trends of activity and membership will serve as the basis for goal-setting for community performance. Understanding how many members join the community each month as a baseline will give your community management team a goal for how many more you want to join going forward.

Once again, it's important to set your context when measuring community health. A community for a popular consumer item will grow much faster than one for a very specific B2B application or product. In the case of B2B, customer coverage should be considered as well. In other words, what percentage of my current customer set belongs to my community? What percentage do you consider to be a success? If you have only 1500 customers, chance are you won't have much more than 1500 members unless you have more than one member per customer (in which case membership needs to be considered by customer company as well as by individual member). Community activity can be considered in a similar manner: What is your expectation for healthy activity? You can begin to understand where you want to be only by understanding the baseline activity that you have as well as the context for the activity. Are users posting only when they have problems? Are they posting new ways to use your product, ideas, or other comments? Does the community have an identity? Are the users identified? Are there leaders? All of these attributes will contribute to setting the context for your community activity.

For the second area of focus—how analytics can tie into and support other business goals across the company—it is important that community management not be an isolated outlier but have exposure across the company. Community analytics is a direct line to the oracular Voice of the Customer. Every business unit from marketing and sales to customer support should be paying attention to your customer dialogue. Getting that to happen may depend on executive sponsorship and advocacy but, once those business units are paying attention, be prepared for an onslaught of reporting questions.

Under the pressure of heightened attention, be careful not to let the metrics distract your community management team from its primary focus. What is your customer coverage by region? How many answers are happening per month? Who are the product evangelists and who are the product detractors? What are the popular topics or enhancement requests for your products? What are the most common problems with your products? The metrics you collect can provide insight into these and many other questions related to your company's overall business strategy and goals.

Give yourself time to digest what metrics your community has to offer. It is easy to become overwhelmed once the requests begin coming. But if you can prepare and understand what the possibilities are, then you will be better able to work with the internal stakeholders and pull reports that support their goals.

Once this process starts, the blocks come off and the communities can become an integral part of the complete customer lifecycle. Understanding what works and what doesn't, warning signs, and evidence of success can help you build a blueprint for successful communities and successful customer experience. Often the metrics that allow one business unit to analyze its efforts will translate to another business unit—at least in the sense that the techniques will be transferable. It is important to codify these best practices and replicate the feedback loop between customer and business goals throughout the enterprise.

Summary

Measurement can make the community. By accurately tracking and understanding your community and its trends you can assess the health of the community, determine where it needs to go, and align its success with that of business goals across your company. The metrics that will be available to you may be platform-dependent, but there are common measures that fall into categories such as population, activity, and value. Your business needs will determine the format and frequency in which these are delivered.

Your business needs also drive what tools you use to report. If you are delivering periodic reports, Microsoft Excel may suffice. But if you are reporting across multiple platforms, then you may need more sophisticated tools such as mashup reporting tools or an enterprise data warehouse. Likewise, if you are measuring and reporting on lists and counts for your metrics, you can achieve that with spreadsheets and databases. But if you are looking for deep data analysis of the unstructured data in your community forums, you will need specialized tools for collection and processing.

As always, being prepared will help ensure success. Setting a baseline and understanding the context of your metrics will support your efforts to explain the results to your executive sponsorship and quantify the value the community health has to other business units. All levels of your company need continual proofs of the proposition that your communities give you unparalleled access to your company's most valuable asset—your customers.

Index

A, B

Big data, 178
Big launch, 73
Blogs, 32

C

Call deflection
    Petouhoff method, 136
    simplest method, 137
    TSIA method, 135
CA technologies, 77, 88
    Facebook page, 115
    follow-up, 116
    history, 116
    marketing/education site, 116
    product support forum, 116
    social suite solution, 117
    success measurements, 127
    users
        listening, 119
        motivation (see Motivation)
        support, 119
Chat, 32
Code sharing, 32
Commander's Intent (CI), 80
Community business return measurement
    business goals, 180
    community metrics, 161
    median, 163
    metrics
        answer, 166
        likes/ratings, 166

polls, 167
post count, 165
surveys, 167
text mining, 168
user population, 165
View count/page view, 164
visits count, 164
mode, 163
reporting
    ad hoc, 169
    bubble chart, 172
    CA product, 171
    dashboard, 173
    infographics, 173
    periodic, 169
    posts vs. active threads, 170
    scatterplot chart, 171
tools
    big data, 178
    databases, 175
    enterprise data warehouse, 176
    mashup, 176
    pitfalls, 178
    social graphing, 177
    spreadsheet, 174
    text mining, 176
valuable, usable, and engaging, 161
Community engagement model, 125
Community Leadership Summit (CLS), 84
Community life cycle model
    community roundtable model
        community management, 80
        content and programming, 81
        culture, 80

Community life cycle model (*cont.*)
    leadership, 79
    metrics and measurement, 83
    policies and governance, 82
    strategy, 79
    tools, 82
  established state, 75
  mature state, 76
  mitotic state, 77
  onboarding state, 73

Community management, 80, 89
  active community management, 92
  capital investment
    digital capitalization, 90
    influence, pillars of, 90
    tangible and quantifiable, 91
    trust factor, 91
  car-racing analogy, 102
    car chief/engineers, 103
    content contribution, 104
    crew chief/mechanics, 103
    driver/car, 103
    fans, 103
    owner, 102
    pit crew, 103
    sponsor, 102
    team manager, 103
  in CA Technologies, 94
  desirable traits, 95
    depth of experience, 96
    empathy, 98
    entrepreneurial
      spirit/resourcefulness, 96
    flexibility, 97
    nonjudgmental, 98
    passion/affinity, 95
    personality, 97
  failed communities, 108
    business needs, 112
    dedicated community, lack of, 109
    fact/fiction, 109
    lack of content, 110
    reasons, 108
    technology platform, 111
    uninteresting topic, 109
  interview process, 101
  passive community management, 91
  principles, 106

  pros and cons, 99
  vendors and customers, 100
Community maturity assessment
  CA Technologies scheme, 87
  radar chart, 84–85
  spidergram, 85–86
  traffic-light visualization reports, 83–84
Community models
  CA technologies, 62–63
  finance model
    determination, 66
    fee-based model, 65
    hybrid model, 66
    internally-funded, 65
    online community, 66
    organization, 65
    ROI, 66
  governance (see Governance models)
  privacy (see Privacy models)
Community planning
  capabilities, 31–32
  components, 31
  financial funding, 36
  off-domain structure, 35
  on-domain structure, 35
  participation value, 31
  strategy decisions, 25–26
  target audience
    CA Technologies, online
      communities, 27
    educational communities, 26
    informal assessment, 28
    innovation-focused communities, 29
    interests, 27
    language barriers and cultural
      differences, 27
    leadership community, 26
    professional communities, 29
    professional consulting services, 27
    social maturity, 30
    strategy/thought leadership
      communities, 29
    technical support communities, 28
  technical platform, online community, 35
  use and design, 35
Community strategy, 79
Competition, 1, 13

Content and programming, 81

Crowdsourcing
blogs, 138
ideas, 138
ideation measurement, 139
message board, 138
product management, 139
public ideation system, 139

Culture, 80

Culture of transparency
blogs, 150
customer trust and loyalty, 151
ideas, 151
measurement
sentiment, 152
surveys, 152
message boards, 150
social networks, 151

Customer engagement
B2B *vs.* B2C communities, 18
consideration chart, 44
customer satisfaction scores, 18
end user functionality, 43
online community (*see* Online
community)
professional communities, 19
social media, 17
successful community (*see* Successful
community)

Customer relationship management (CRM)
system, 49, 140
badging, 142
community member role, 142
personalization, 142
profiles, 141
ranking, 142
registration process, 141
social data measurement, 143

D

Document libraries, 32

E, F

Established community, 73

G, H

Gamification, 41, 121

Governance models
control-to-advocacy range, 56
external community
altruistic/pay-it-forward reasons, 60
balance of influence, 59
CA technologies, 60
influence of, 58
information challenge exists, 59
principles of, 61
protecting, 58
relationship, 58
role of advocate, 61
hive-mind/wild-wild-West
environments, 56
hybrid, 61, 65
influence, 55
internal governance, 57
online community, 55
responsibility, 55
tradeoff, 56

I, J, K

Ideation, 32

Innovation-focused communities, 29

Intelligent data operating layer (IDOL), 177

L

Leadership, 79

M

Mature community, 75

Message boards, 31

Metcalfe's law, 72

Metrics and measurement, 83

Mitotic community, 76

Motivation
accepted solutions, 122
application performance
management community, 121
badging system, 121

Motivation (*cont.*)
  community engagement model, 125
  gamification, 121
  membership, 126
  MyCA, 125
  near-triple-digit percentage, 122
  reward-and-motivation system, 120

MyCA
  community landing page, 122–123
  mentor program, 125
  rock stars, 125
  RSS, 125
  social sharing, 125
  surveys, polls and functions, 122
  technical users, 125
  user page, 122, 124

N

NodeXL, 177

Non-disclosure agreement (NDA), 50

O

Off-domain structure, 35

Onboarding community, 72

On-domain structure, 35

Online communities
  community focus, 132
  CRM system (see Customer relationship
    management (CRM) system)
  crowdsourcing (see Crowdsourcing)
  culture of transparency (see Culture of
    transparency)
  customer retention and loyalty, 143
  customer services costs reducing
    blogs, 134
    call deflection (see Call deflection)
    documentation and knowledge base
      systems improvement, 135
    e-mail newsletters and
      subscriptions, 134
    message boards, 134
    peer-to-peer support, 133
    question-and-answer process, 133
    social network engagement, 134
  direct business outcomes, 133
  indirect outcomes, 133

social business maturity, 153
thought leadership (see Thought leadership)

Online community, 18
  capabilities, 41
  gamification, 41
  social channels, 40

Online product community
  business plan, 14–15
  competition, 1, 13
  humans
    communication, 4
    communities of purpose, 2
    community and society
      relationship, 4
    justify an investment, 12
    neurotransmitters, 5–6
    nucleus accumbens and
      dopamine regulation, 6
    oxytocin and trust, 9
    social bonds, 3
    technology, 11
  return on investment (ROI), 1, 12
  social networking, 1, 13

Open database connectivity (ODBC), 176

P, Q

Petouhoff method, 136

Policies and governance, 82

Population metrics, 165

Privacy models
  access levels, 48
  hybrid community, 53
  private community
    benefit, 52
    customer advisory boards, 52
    development, 52
    features, 53
    gated content, 51
    industry-specific groups, 52
    life cycle, 53
    mass adoption, 52
    supporting, 52
    trust, 52
  public community
    collaboration, 51
    definition, 48

economic value, 49
education, 51
goals, 50
key factor, 50
large/small community, 49
leadership, 51
monitoring, 51
networking and CRM, 49
organization, 50
search engines, 49
self-service model, 49
social channels, 48
supporting, 51
types of content, 50
Professional communities, 29

R

Radar chart, 84

Real simple syndication (RSS), 125

Regional user group, 77

Return on investment (ROI), 1, 12, 66

Return on the investment (ROI), 75–76

90/9/1 rule, 74

S

Search engine optimization (SEO), 49, 164

Simplest method, 137

Social channel integration, 32

Social media, 40

Social networking, 1, 13

Soft launch, 73

Software as a service (SaaS), 82

Special interest groups (SIGs), 77

Spidergram, 84–85

Spreadsheets, 174

Strategy/thought leadership communities, 29

Structure query language (SQL), 175

Successful community
  business planning
    decision considerations, 23
    supporting company goals, 22
  community planning (see Community
    planning)

continuous improvement, 39
decision making, 24
due diligence
  additional value, 22
  customers participation, 21
  education team, 20
  executive management, 21
  marketing department, 20
  members benefit, 21
  partner program team, 21
  product development group, 21
  product management team, 21
  professional services team, 21
  technical support, 20
  understanding business and
    community, 20
launching, 37
monitor, sustain, and success
  evaluation, 38
opening activities, 37

T, U

Technical support communities, 28

Technology services industry association
  (TSIA) method, 135

Thought leadership
  blogs, 145
  customers trust, 147
  measurement
    comments, 148
    ratings, 148
    shares, 148
    views, 147
    visitors, 147
  message boards, 145
  newsletters, 146
  wikis, 146

Traffic-light visualization report, 83–84

V

Video libraries, 32

W, X, Y, Z

Webcasts/podcasts, 32

Wikis, 32

31901055205738

CPSIA information can be obtained at www.ICGtesting.com
Printed in the USA
LVOW08s2142180913

353114LV00005B/154/P